D0517796

History Alive
4

1900—1970s

Peter Moss

Illustrated by George B. Hamilton

Collins Educational

© Peter Moss 1967, 1977
First published in Great Britain 1967 by Blond Educational. Reprinted 1968, 1969, 1970. Revised edition 1972.
Reprinted 1973, 1974 (twice), 1975.
Second edition 1977, reprinted 1978, 1979, 1980, 1982,
published by Hart-Davis Educational Ltd
a division of Granada Publishing
Frogmore, St Albans, Hertfordshire
Reprinted by COLLINS EDUCATIONAL 1984

Collins Publishing

ISBN 0 247 12792 2

All rights reserved. No part of this publication may be reproduced, stored in a retrieval system, or transmitted, in any form or by any means, electronic, mechanical, photocopying, recording or otherwise, without the prior permission of the publishers.

Printed in Great Britain by Butler & Tanner Ltd, Frome and London.

Introductory Book	55BC–1485
Book 1	1485–1714
Book 2	1688–1789
Book 3	1789–1914
Book 4	1900–1970s

This series, planned to cover the C.S.E. syllabus in depth, gains its delightfully fresh approach by combining a fluid and vivid text with an amusing and highly original style of illustration.

ACKNOWLEDGEMENTS
The author and publisher wish to thank the following: Gibbs and Phillips Ltd. for the extracts from *The War Despatches* of Sir Philip Gibbs; B.T. Batsford Ltd. for the extract from *The Battle of Jutland*, by G. Bennett; J.M. Dent & Sons Ltd. for the extracts from *Coco the Clown*, by N. Poliakoff; Macmillan & Co. Ltd. for the extract from *The Last Enemy*, by R. Hillary; Victor Gollancz Ltd. for the extracts from *Hiroshima Diary*, by Michihiko Hachiya; Oxford University Press for the extract from *Resurrection*, by L. Tolstoy (tr. L. Maude).

Series cover design by Lyon Benzimra

Contents

THE SOCIAL CLASSES 1900-1914

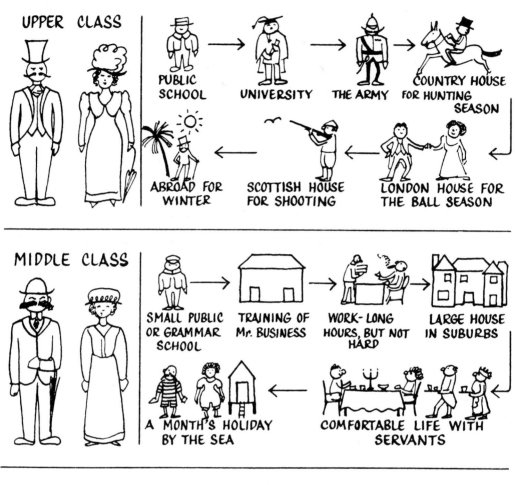

UPPER CLASS

PUBLIC SCHOOL → UNIVERSITY → THE ARMY → COUNTRY HOUSE FOR HUNTING SEASON

ABROAD FOR WINTER ← SCOTTISH HOUSE FOR SHOOTING ← LONDON HOUSE FOR THE BALL SEASON ←

MIDDLE CLASS

SMALL PUBLIC OR GRAMMAR SCHOOL → TRAINING OF Mr. BUSINESS → WORK- LONG HOURS, BUT NOT HARD → LARGE HOUSE IN SUBURBS

A MONTH'S HOLIDAY BY THE SEA ← COMFORTABLE LIFE WITH SERVANTS ←

WORKING CLASS

BOARD SCHOOL UNTIL 12 (or later) → WORK AT 12-14 → LONG HOURS → LOW WAGES

DREAD OF UNEMPLOYMENT, SICKNESS AND POVERTY IN OLD AGE ← POOR HOUSES ←

1

LIFE IN THE EDWARDIAN AGE
1901–1914

OW THE CLASSES
ERE DIVIDED

BELOW
£160
A YEAR

OVER
2,000,000
FAMILIES
IN
POVERTY

£160-£400
A YEAR

VER £400
A YEAR

UPPER
CLASS

MIDDLE
CLASS

WORKING
CLASS

Although in the first years of the twentieth century the people of England were not as sharply divided into classes as they had been in Victorian times, the divisions between the upper, middle and working classes were much more clearly marked than they are today. In the second half of the twentieth century the lives of the factory worker or the shop assistant and the managing director of the firm for which he works are really very similar: fifty years ago they would have been completely different. It was possible for a man to rise in life through hard work, intelligence or pure luck, but most people remained in the group in which they had been born.

AVERAGE AGE OF DEATHS
IN LONDON, 1906

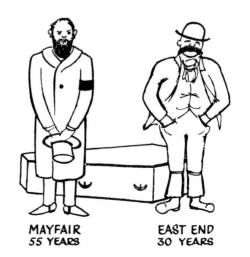

MAYFAIR
55 YEARS

EAST END
30 YEARS

The upper class, whose large income came mainly from the rents of land and property, lived very pleasant lives, with large houses and many servants. Their children had a long and leisurely education, starting under governesses at home, followed, for the boys at least, by a period at an important public school and then a few years at Oxford or Cambridge. Girls often remained with their governesses and tutors until their teens, but more were beginning to go to expensive boarding schools, and a few even went to the university.

After finishing their education, the young men usually had no need to work unless they wanted to. If they felt that they had to do something, then the army or navy, the Church, or politics were considered respectable careers as Members of Parliament received no payment at all until 1911, and to be an officer in the army or navy cost far more than the pay given. It was still considered not quite 'proper' for a gentleman to have to work for money. A young man might enter the family business if there was one—at the top, of course—or else help in the running of the family estates. Girls, after a few years of attending balls, usually married a wealthy young man a few years older than themselves, and settled down to the normal life of the upper class, which was largely made up of amusements.

In the spring they would move to their country houses: the summer would be spent in the London home for the season of balls, operas, theatres and sporting events: the autumn would see them in their Scottish estate or Highland hotel for the shooting and fishing: winter was often spent abroad travelling in a warmer climate. It was very pleasant to be a member of the upper class.

A typical breakfast menu of a wealthy family in 1905
Porridge; omelet with kidneys or ham; eggs—poached or baked; fish—cod, whiting; cold chicken; potted meat; rolls, toast, bread; jam, marmalade, butter; tea, coffee.

(One need not, of course, have everything.)

The middle classes—wealthy tradesmen, businessmen, doctors, lawyers and other professional men—also lived comfortable lives, even if they did have to work daily for their living. The hours of work in office or factory may have been long, but on the whole it was not hard and there were always employees to do whatever was asked. The middle-class home was usually a large, solid house in the suburbs, with several servants and all the latest comforts—perhaps, even, one of the new-fangled motor cars. Although the life of a middle class family was not one round of pleasure, they did have a fair amount of leisure. They usually had a whole month at the seaside in the summer at an hotel or, more often, in a house rented for the season. Sometimes there would be holidays on the continent, and throughout the year there would be weekends in the country at their own cottage or with friends, for shooting, fishing and hunting. The women of the middle class, like those of the upper class, never went to work, but kept themselves busy running the home, the servants, their social life and helping in church bazaars and other charities.

The ordinary working-class family lived a very different life. The average wage of a working man in 1901 was 85p—£1 a week, though a highly skilled man would get as much as £2. Their homes were often in poor terraced slums or in big blocks of tenements left over from the nineteenth century. They had, of course, no servants—it was the wives and children of the working class who were the servants of the middle and upper classes. The hours of work were long—ten hours a day from Monday to Friday, and six and a half on Saturday. In shops the day was even longer for the shops did not close until seven o'clock or even later in the evening, but by law every assistant did have to be allowed one free half day a week, usually Wednesday afternoon. Wages could still be kept low as there were plenty of men without jobs ready to take those of anyone who asked for higher wages for although the trade unions were growing rapidly, especially among lower-paid people, they did not have the power they have today.

1850	1880-1890's	1890's-1910

CRAFT UNIONS	RISE OF UNSKILLED UNIONS	THE UNIONS TAKE TO POLITICS

Until the 1870s unions were, on the whole, small, and successful only among the highly-skilled, highly-paid craftsmen who could afford large union subscriptions and who could bring the whole factory to a standstill if they went on strike. Clerical workers, and unskilled men such as dockers and labourers were difficult to organise, as they could not afford to pay much to a union, and were, in any case, very easy to replace if they went on strike. Even the craft unions (e.g. carpenters, engineers) had to fight individually for what they wanted: if one factory or trade managed to obtain higher wages, it did not mean that all other factories or similar trades were given the same rate. It was a case of every union and every factory for itself.

Towards the end of the nineteenth century and during the first years of the twentieth a change began to come over the trade unions. First of all unskilled men and women began to band together to form unions which grew in power, and secondly, the unions began to realise that fighting the employers one at a time, and factory by factory was a waste of time and effort. If they could send members to parliament to put the working man's case they might be able to have the laws of the country changed so that improved conditions would apply to all workers and factories at the same time. To this end the ILP (Independent Labour Party) was formed, and beginning with 3 ILP M.P.s in 1893, representation increased rapidly as shown below. (The Labour Party came into existence in 1900.)

How the unions and the Labour Party increased side by side

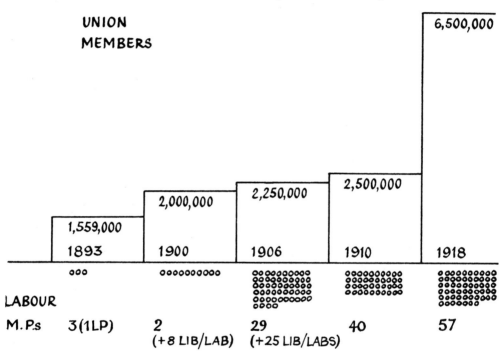

Although the foundations of the power of the trade unions and the Labour Party were being firmly laid in the early years of the twentieth century, before 1914 they had not yet enough strength to do all they wanted, especially about conditions of work. Working people were usually allowed only a week's or a fortnight's holiday a year, together with Bank holidays, often without pay. Holidays were not welcome, however, for with wages so low the working class could rarely afford to go away, and all that most of them could afford were trips to the local amusements or a cheap day excursion by train to the nearest seaside resort. Other luxuries were rare too for working people since every family had to try to save a little money in case of unemployment or sickness (until 1911 there was no government help for

8

men who were out of work or ill) and for their old age (Old Age pensions were not introduced until 1908).

Here are two typical diets of working class families in 1905. The first is of a foreman earning £1·90 a week, which was a good wage for the time. There were seven in family:

Breakfast: toast, tea.

Dinner: soup, dumplings, meat, bread, tea.

Tea: sardines, bread, milk, tea.

Supper: bread, cheese, cocoa.

This family spent 16p each a week on food, which left 78p for rent, clothes, coal, lighting, amusement and emergencies such as illness. The second is the diet of a poor manual labourer earning 87½p a week. This man had a wife and 3 children.

Breakfast: bread, butter, tea.

Dinner: fish (probably herrings), bread, tea.

Tea: bread, butter, onions, tea.

Supper: none.

Compare this with the typical upper class breakfast menu on page 6.

The great difference between the rich and the poor is shown by the timetable of an ordinary day in the life of a housemaid and that of her mistress.

	Maid		**Mistress**
a.m. 6.30	Clean grates, blacklead them; start cleaning house; heat water and take it to the family's bed-rooms.	**a.m. 8.0**	Get up; breakfast.
8.0	Help prepare and serve breakfast.	**9.0**	Give orders for the day— say what meals wanted and how many guests. Supervise cooking and cleaning (though not touch any herself).
9.0	Get orders for the day; clean upstairs and down; general tidying up.	**11.0**	Visit shops or friends.
11.0	Help Cook to prepare and cook lunch.	**p.m. 1.0**	Lunch, followed by visits, reading, embroidery.
p.m. 1.30	Help serve lunch.		
2.0	Clear away; wash up; finish tidying house; polish silver and cutlery; ironing; mending.	**3.30**	Afternoon tea, entertaining friends, or visiting friends for tea.
3.30	Prepare, serve and clear away tea.	**5.30**	Supervise arrangements for dinner.
5.30	Start preparing dinner. Help Cook.	**6.30**	Dress for dinner.
7.30	Help serve dinner, clear away, wash up.	**7.30**	Dinner, followed by talking, songs in the drawing room, dancing or outside amusement.

Maid	**Mistress**
9.30 Check fires, prepare house for the night.	**11.0–2.0** a.m. Bed, time depending on the company and how the evening was spent.
10.30 Bed, unless the family have a party and need late supper.	

For all of this work the maid would be paid between 25 and 37 pence a week. She would have one half day, or perhaps one evening free a week. Children of twelve and over could go to school for half a day only and work as servants for the other half provided they did not do more than $27\frac{1}{2}$ hours a week (but this was rarely checked). For this they would receive $12\frac{1}{2}$ or 15 pence.

Mistresses sometimes bought some of the clothing for servants who lived in the house. Here is part of an advertisement from a paper of 1908:

Cheap clothing suitable for Servants

Vests	$3\frac{3}{4}$d each. ($1\frac{1}{2}$p)
Petticoat	1/6$\frac{3}{4}$d. each (8p)
Stockings	1/9 for two pairs. (9p)
Non-creaking shoes	2/11 a pair. ($14\frac{1}{2}$p)

Discoveries and inventions in the Edwardian Age

The Edwardian Age (1901–1914) was the end of a long period of British history. A few rich were too rich: many poor were too poor. This was how society had been for centuries, but at the beginning of the twentieth century there was a difference—everyone was now being educated, and the machine was taking over much of the work from man's muscles. In four fields particularly, the discoveries which were made in the Edwardian Age, or just before it, were to help immensely in turning the old way of life upside-down and in making the twentieth century the Age of the Ordinary Man.

Aeroplane (1903)

Motor car (developed 1880's–1890's)

Transport. The motor car began to become an important toy for rich people. There were about 132,000 cars in Britain by 1914. The aeroplane was considered a dangerous freak until the war of 1914, when it was developed for military uses.

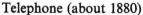

Telephone (about 1880)   Wireless (about 1900)

Communications. The use of the telephone grew rapidly between cities and even countries. Wireless began to be used—not by the public, but only by the Navy, shipping firms and the Post Office. This speeded up news and business, and made life in general move more quickly.

Vacuum cleaner and electricity

Labour-saving inventions. Inventions such as vacuum cleaners, electric irons and lighting, were based on the growing use of electricity. Most cooking and heating was still by coal, though gas cookers were beginning to become popular. These inventions helped to reduce the number of servants needed.

Gramophone (1880–90)   Cinema (1890–1900)

Amusements. Up to this period people had to make their own amusements. The invention of mechanical entertainments, though they were not very widespread until after the war of 1914–18, made cheap amusement available to all classes of people.

11

1. Look at the chart of family incomes on page 5. Every 5 mm in height represents 167,000 families.Measure each column and work out how many families fell into each group.
2. The drawing on page 5 shows that the average age of death in Mayfair (the wealthy part of London) was 55 years, and that in the East End (the poor area) was 30 years. Give as many reasons as you can for this.
3. Why were working people unable to make full use of their holidays?
4. What do you think is the most important kind of food missing from the diets of working people given on page 9? Why do you think they did not eat much of this kind of foodstuff?
5. The average wage in 1976 is about £73 a week—that is, 73 times as much as in 1905. Look at the prices of clothing given on page 10, and multiply each one by 73. How do these figures compare with the prices of these garments today? What expenses do people have today they did not have in 1905?
6. How do you think the inventions mentioned on pages 10 and 11 have helped to break down the barriers between the classes in England?
7. Copy pictures of cars, aeroplanes and fashions of the period 1900–1914 from books in the library to make a wall magazine. Place drawings or photographs of modern machines or clothes by the side to show the differences. Which aspects of these have changed most, and which least?
8. Why were working people so afraid of growing old, of falling ill and of losing their jobs in the first half of this period?
9. Fifty years ago the lives of the factory worker and the managing director would have been very different. Make two columns and list as many differences as you can, e.g.,

Managing director	**Factory worker**
1. Large detatched house.	Terrace or tenement house.

10. Library work: find out from an encyclopaedia what part the following played in England between 1900 and 1914:

(a) David Lloyd George.
(b) Mrs. Pankhurst.
(c) Marconi.
(d) M. Blériot.
(e) Fabian Society.
(f) Winston Churchill.
(g) Ben Tillett.
(h) Keir Hardy.

2

EUROPE SLIDES
INTO WORLD WAR 1

Wars, like quarrels between people, do not usually flare up suddenly. Normally there is long-standing bad-feeling, and then one small incident suddenly turns the hatred into actual fighting. So it was with World War 1, and the causes reached back many years before 1914.

As Germany had become a united country only in 1871, she had not taken part in the scramble for colonies as most of the other European countries had done. Britain and France especially had seized vast areas of land all over the world, and Holland, Spain, Portugal and Belgium also had extensive colonies. By the time the new country of Germany was ready, most of the unoccupied land had already been taken, so that all she could get were some tiny islands in the Pacific Ocean and parts of Africa which were at the time unprofitable. Mighty Germany, the third largest country in Europe, had only half as many people in her colonies as tiny Holland had in hers.

BRITISH COLONIES 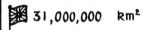 31,000,000 km²   400,000,000 PEOPLE

FRENCH COLONIES 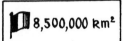 8,500,000 km²   26,000,000 PEOPLE

GERMAN COLONIES 2,590,000 km² (MUCH OF IT UNPROFITABLE)
12,000,000 PEOPLE

In the last twenty-five years of the nineteenth century Germany had become a great industrial country, with great coal mines, chemical works and factories turning out every type of product, but especially ships, engines, machinery and weapons. This meant there was great rivalry for trade, particularly with Britain who had half a century's start in industry and was well established in the foreign markets. Production of everything in Germany soared.

From the beginning of the century there was a race in armament building for the war which most people thought was bound to come sooner or

13

German Production

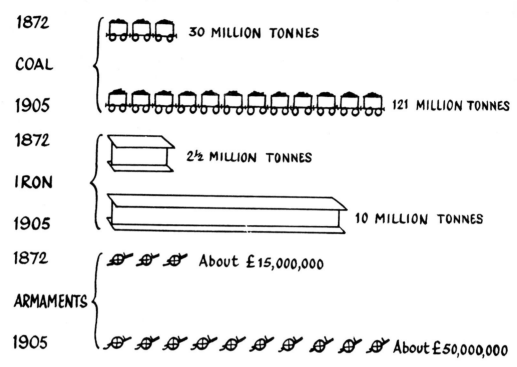

1872 COAL ⎰ 30 MILLION TONNES

1905 ⎱ 121 MILLION TONNES

1872 IRON ⎰ 2½ MILLION TONNES

1905 ⎱ 10 MILLION TONNES

1872 ARMAMENTS ⎰ About £15,000,000

1905 ⎱ About £50,000,000

later. France and Germany struggled to outdo each other in the size of their armies, the number of guns and the strength of their fortresses, while Britain and Germany raced to build the bigger navy. Bigger, faster and more-heavily armed ships followed one after another in the effort to win command of the seas when war came.

Meanwhile, the countries of Europe were taking sides and forming alliances. Germany, Austria and Italy (who later changed sides) formed the centre of one group: Russia and France were the centre of the rival group. Although Britain did not actually sign a treaty as the other countries had done, it was fairly certain that in the event of war she would help France and Russia. The scene was now set for the showdown: the two heavily armed groups were ready for war. Germany thought that Russia might be the weak link on her enemies' side, for Russia had been badly defeated by Japan in 1905 and looked ready for a revolution. All Germany needed was an excuse, and in June, 1914, this was given to her.

An Austrian prince, Archduke Franz Ferdinand, was shot dead in his car while on a visit to the small Austrian possession of Bosnia, which was friendly with Russia. Almost without waiting for an explanation, Austria, who feared Serbian attempts to wrest Bosnia from her, attacked Serbia, who called to her ally, Russia, for help. Germany declared war to help her

GERMANY HAD FEW COLONIES

ARMS RACE ÷ NAVY: BRITAIN-GERMANY
ARMY: FRANCE-GERMANY

1880

1900

GERMANY SUDDENLY A POWERFUL, WEALTHY, INDUSTRIAL COUNTRY

1910

EUROPA

1914

COUNTRIES OF EUROPE FORMED RIVAL GROUPS

MURDER OF ARCHDUKE FRANZ FERDINAND

friends, the Austrians, and France joined in to support her ally, Russia. Ignoring the protests of the Belgian government, the Germans invaded Belgium, which had been a neutral country for seventy-five years, to attack Northern France. Within a few days Britain had joined France and Russia, and the war had begun in earnest. Although Europe did not know it, the old way of life that had taken centuries to build up, had gone for ever: four years of the bitterest, bloodiest and most expensive fighting ever known was going to change completely the map of Europe, men's ideas, and the history of the world.

THE MAIN BATTLEFIELDS OF WORLD WAR I

Final line-up for the War

Britain and her Empire.
France.
Belgium.
Italy. (after 1915)
Serbia.
Roumania. (after 1916)
Portugal. (after 1916)
Russia. (until 1917)
U.S.A. (after 1917)
Japan.

V.

Germany.
Austria.
Hungary.
Turkey.
Bulgaria. (after 1915)

---

1. Imagine Britain, France, Germany, Russia, Austria and Serbia were in an international court charged with being responsible for World War 1. Give the main points of evidence lawyers for the prosecution and the defence could bring for each country. If you were a judge deciding the case, which of the defendants would you find guilty?
2. Why do you think Britain was particularly anxious when Germany began to build a powerful navy? (Look at your map from question 1.)
3. Why should France and Germany compete to build the bigger army, and why should Britain and Germany compete to build the bigger navy?
4. Look at the charts of Germany's increase in production between 1872 and 1905. By how many times, approximately, did her output increase?
5. Find the former German colonies on an atlas. Find out what kind of countries they were (climate, vegetation etc.) and why other European countries had not colonised them.
6. Encyclopaedia work: Look up in the Oxford Junior Encyclopaedia and find out when the following were added to the British Empire and who was mainly responsible: Australia, Canada, New Zealand, South Africa, Nigeria, India, Malaya, Burma and Rhodesia.

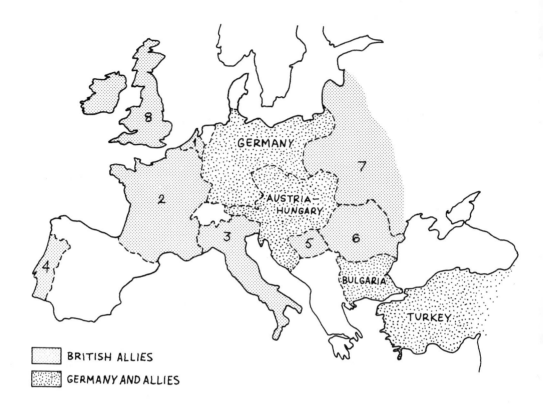

BRITISH ALLIES

GERMANY AND ALLIES

7. Write down the names of the countries represented by the figures 1–7 on the map (5 is Serbia which no longer exists as a separate country but is part of Yugoslavia). Countries 1, 2, 3, 5, 6, and 7 appear to surround Germany and Austria and to separate them from their allies, Turkey and Bulgaria. The main enemy, however, was Germany and Austria. In what ways do you think the allies of Britain were at a disadvantage by being scattered all round the compact block of Germany and Austria?

3

WORLD WAR 1 1914-1918

When war broke out in 1914 most of the people in Europe were pleased. War seemed rather exciting and glamorous, with gallant young men dashing into battle—preferably on horseback, of course—waving swords and flags. Four years later these dreams had vanished and a bitterly disillusioned Europe, with ten million of its best men dead, realised the true cruelty of modern war. There was no glamour here—nothing but stark horror, misery and tragedy.

There had been no major war in Europe for a century, and great changes had taken place in fighting methods. Science, engineering and all the resources of the industry that had developed during the nineteenth century were thrown into the battle for quicker ways of killing more and more men, and of doing more and more damage. The latest inventions, the motor engine, aeroplanes and wireless, unreliable and crude in 1914, soon developed under war conditions into efficient fighting machines. As the struggle went on, motor vehicles, which in pre-war days had been rare except in cities, and which were little more than a novelty for the wealthy, gradually drove out the horse as transport, and developed lethal sidelines such as tanks and self-propelled guns. The flying machine, which in 1914 was still a mad toy for mad men, soon established itself as a fighting machine, growing faster and faster, more lethal and less liable to crash. It was soon found too, that wireless, which was scarcely out of its laboratory, could be handled and operated by ordinary men on the battlefield. This too, grew more efficient and more reliable as the war dragged on.

In the actual fighting, instead of great cavalry charges by cheering, shouting soldiers, the armies of 1914 dug trenches in the earth, protected them with sandbags and barbed wire, and filled them with men armed with rifles, machine guns and hand grenades. Fifty, a hundred or two hundred metres away, the enemy did the same, and the object was to wipe out the men in the opposing trench by any possible means, and to capture the ground they defended.

Day and night heavy guns, made in the great new engineering factories and powered by the scientists' latest explosives, a hundred times more destructive than the simple gunpowder of previous wars, hurled thousands of tons of shells towards the enemy to blow him to bits. Tanks, after 1916, crawled through the enemy's barbed wire to crush him or shoot him to death: poison gas was poured from one trench to another when the wind was in the right direction to blind and suffocate with appalling suffering: machines hurled out jets of roaring flame, and when all other methods failed, there was still the old-fashioned rifle and bayonet to spear him.

The land for far around the front line trenches became a dead world—apart from the miserable living men who crouched in the shelter of the earth ditches. Grass, trees, houses—everything disappeared into a chaos of wreckage and rotting human remains lying in a sea of mud in winter and a bed of dust in summer.

Month after month, year after year, men battled out the war under indescribable hardships of mud, water, filth and fear. For the loss of fifty thousand men they might move forward one week and gain a few hundred metres of churned-up, useless ground: a fortnight later, for the loss of even more men, they might lose it again. For the whole four years of the war, the battle lines on the Western Front (Northern France and Belgium) where most of the fighting was done, did not move more than a few kilometres.

At sea it was much the same story. There was one great battle in which the fleets of Britain and Germany met face to face in the manner of Trafalgar (the battle of Jutland), but all the while submarines prowled beneath the waves ready to torpedo any enemy ship, armed or unarmed. Mines were sprinkled throughout the sea lanes to destroy anything, enemy or neutral, warship, merchant ship, passenger liner or even hospital ships. In the air, the early aeroplanes twisted and turned to spot enemy troop movements so that the men on the ground could know when to attack and when to retreat. Later on, the planes took to fighting their own little war in the air, and towards the end of the fighting a few German airships and some heavy bombing aeroplanes managed to reach England. Although their bombs were small and they did relatively little damage, they gave a terrifying foretaste of what might be to come.

The struggle was so grim, and the slaughter so great, that the British government could no longer rely on men volunteering to fight, and in 1916 conscription was introduced for the first time. Now every fit man, the willing and the unwilling, the brave and the cowardly, was forced to join one of the fighting forces unless he was in a vitally important job. And when the supply was still not enough, women 'soldiers' and 'sailors' were brought in to do such duties as driving, office work and cooking so that the men could be released for actual fighting.

So, when the last shot was fired on November 11th, 1918, the whole of Europe was so revolted by the horrors of the four years of destruction that everyone determined that this, the Great War, should be the last of wars—the 'war to end all wars' as they called it. Peace for ever, they said, had been bought with those ten million lives and countless millions of pounds of damage. If only they could have seen that within twenty-one years another war was to break out which would take five times as many lives as 'their' war!

20

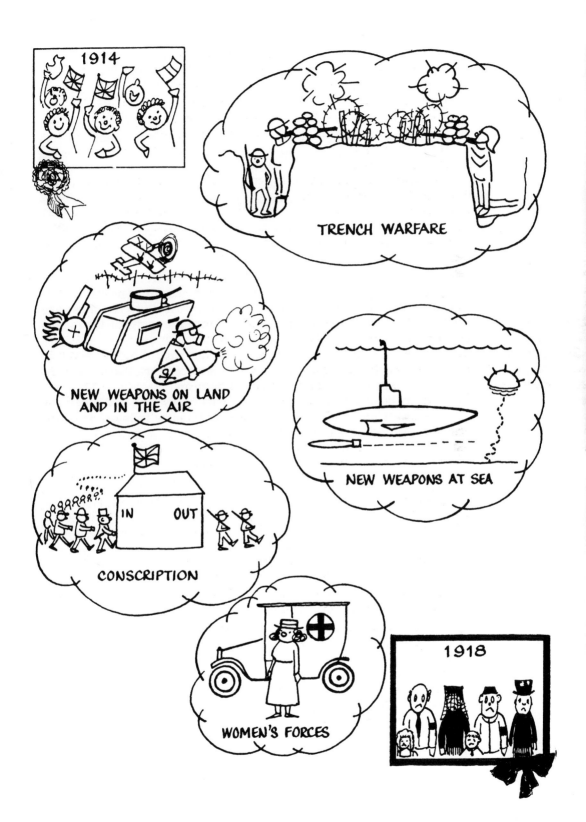

1914

TRENCH WARFARE

NEW WEAPONS ON LAND AND IN THE AIR

NEW WEAPONS AT SEA

IN OUT

CONSCRIPTION

WOMEN'S FORCES

1918

These are extracts from messages sent from the Western Front by Sir Philip Gibbs, war correspondent for the 'Daily Telegraph' and other papers.

Tanks

"But we had a new engine of war to destroy the place. Over our own trenches in the twilight of the dawn one of these motor-monsters had lurched up, and now it came crawling forward to the rescue, cheered by the assaulting troops... *Crème de Menthe* was the name of this particular creature, and it waddled forwards right over the old German trenches and went forward very steadily towards the sugar factory.

There was a second of silence from the enemy there. Then, suddenly, their machine-gun fire burst out in nervous spasms and splashed the sides of *Crème de Menthe*.

But the tank did not mind. The bullets fell from its sides harmlessly. It advanced upon a broken wall, leaned up against it heavily until it fell with a crash of bricks, and then rose on to the bricks and passed over them, and walked straight into the midst of the factory ruins.

From its sides came flashes of fire and a hose of bullets, and then it trampled around over machine-gun emplacements, 'having a grand time', as one of the men said with enthusiasm.

It crushed the machine-guns under its heavy ribs, and killed machine-gun teams with a deadly fire. The Infantry followed in... and then advanced round the flanks of the monster."

Desolation

"In all that broad stretch of desolation we have left behind us the shell-craters which were full of water, red water, and green water, are now dried up, and are hard, deep pits, scooped out of powdered earth, from which all vitality has gone, so that spring brings no life to it. I thought that perhaps some of these shell-slashed woods would put out new shoots when spring came, and watched them curiously for any sign of rebirth, but there is no sign, and their poor, mutilated limbs, their broken and tattered trunks, stand naked under the blue sky. Everything is dead, with a white, ghastly look in the brilliant sunshine,... Dead horses lie on the roadsides or in shell-craters. I passed a row of these poor beasts as though all had fallen down and died together in a last comradeship. Dead Germans or bits of dead Germans, lie in old trenches, and these fields are the graveyards of Youth."

(*The War Despatches*, Sir Philip Gibbs)

This is how a German naval officer describes an incident in the Battle of Jutland, in which the German High Seas Fleet met the British Grand Fleet headlong in the North Sea:

"They (the battleships) hurled themselves recklessly against the enemy line. A dense hail of fire swept them all away. Hit after hit struck our ship. A 15-inch shell pierced the armour of 'Caesar' turret and exploded inside. Lieutenant-Commander von Boltenstern had both legs torn off and nearly the whole gunhouse crew was killed. The shell set on fire two cordite charges from which the flames spread to the transfer chamber where they set fire to four more and from there to the case-chamber where four more ignited. The burning cases emitted great tongues of flame which shot up as high as a house; but they only blazed, they did not explode as had been the case with the enemy. This saved the ship, but killed all but five of the 70 men inside the turret. A few minutes later this catastrophe was followed by a second. A 15-inch shell pierced the roof of 'Dora' turret and the same horrors ensued. With the exception of one man who was thrown by the concussion through the turret entrance, the whole crew of 80 men were killed instantly."

(Von Hase, quoted in *The Battle of Jutland*, by Geoffrey Bennett)

---

1. How was the fighting in World War 1 completely different from that of previous wars?
2. What were the main new weapons used in the war? Which of these do you think turned out to be the most dangerous in the end?
3. What is conscription? Why did it have to be introduced during the war?
4. Draw pictures of a tank of World War 1 and a modern tank, and a World War 1 aeroplane and a modern fighter. Which of the two—tanks or aeroplanes—do you think have developed most in the fifty or sixty years? Why do you think this is so?
5. If a column of men in single file were marching by at a brisk pace—say $6\frac{1}{2}$ km/h—about 7000 would pass in an hour. At least 10,000,000 soldiers died in the war: work out how long these would take to walk past you (answer in weeks, days and hours).
6. Look at your local war memorial, if you have one, and count the number of men killed in the war 1914–1918, and compare it with the number killed in the Second World War. What do you notice most of all?
7. Encyclopaedia work: Find out what happened at the following places during the war: the Somme, Gallipoli, Mons, Tannenberg, Zeebrugge.
8. Who were the following and what did they do during the war: General von Hindenburg, General von Ludendorff, Field Marshal Haig, Marshal Foch, General Allenby, General Pershing, Col. T. E. Lawrence, Count von Zeppelin.

GERMANY MUST PAY FOR THE WAR IN MONEY AND GOODS.

TREATY OF VERSAILLES 1919
① -----
② -----
③ -----
④ -----
‿‿ (Gt.Britain)
‿‿ (France)
‿‿ (U.S.A.)
‿‿ (Italy)

GERMANY TO HAVE NO AIR FORCE OR SUBMARINES. ONLY TINY ARMY AND NAVY.

PACIFIC ISLANDS
WEST AFRICA
EAST AFRICA
S.W. AFRICA

GERMANY TO HAND OVER COLONIES

LEAGUE OF NATIONS SET UP

GERMANY
RUSSIA
TURKEY
AUSTRIA
HUNGARY

PARTS OF COUNTRIES CUT OFF TO MAKE NEW COUNTRIES

4

HOW WORLD WAR 1 WAS SETTLED

The Treaty of Versailles

When the fighting ended on November 11th 1918, representatives of 27 nations, together with delegates from the British Dominions, who had declared war on Germany (not all of them had actually taken part in the fighting) met at Versailles, near Paris, to decide what was to happen to the beaten enemy. The four most important men at the conference, and the ones who really made most of the decisions, were the Prime Ministers of Britain, France and Italy, Mr. Lloyd George, M. Clemenceau and Signor Orlando, and the President of the United States, Mr. Wilson. The Germans were not allowed to send any representatives to put their side of the case—a fact which was to cause a great deal of trouble before many years had passed.

The conference, which began in 1919, decided that Germany was responsible for the war, and must be punished for causing so much damage. She was ordered to pay large sums of money and to give her merchant ships and much of her coal production to the allies who had won the war. In all, the cost to Germany was about six thousand six hundred million pounds, over half of which was to be paid to France who had suffered the most damage. Of course, this sum was impossibly large and very little of it was ever paid.

Next, all of Germany's colonies were taken from her and placed by the League of Nations (pages 28–29) in the care of Britain, France, Belgium, South Africa, Australia and New Zealand. These countries were not given the colonies as possessions, but were made responsible for keeping them in order and developing them into modern states.

In case Germany should ever try to start another war, she was forbidden to have any submarines or military aeroplanes, which were considered the most dangerous weapons. She was allowed to keep only a very small army, and a navy of six battleships of 10,000 tons and some smaller vessels—just enough to keep law and order.

The conference then came to what was considered the most important item—the re-shaping of the map of Europe. In the west, the two 'counties' of Alsace and Lorraine, which Germany had taken from France in the war of 1870 were given back. Belgium and Denmark were also given a small area of Germany. But it was in the east, between Germany and her

Austrian ally and Russia that the greatest changes took place. Two completely 'new' states (Czecho-Slovakia and Yugo-Slavia) were created, and one (Poland) which had been swallowed up by Germany and Russia nearly a hundred years earlier, was given its independence again. Three small states, Estonia, Latvia and Lithuania, were established between 1920 and 1922 from parts of the old Russian Empire on the eastern shore of the Baltic Sea.

As far as possible the statesmen tried to make for the different races of this part of the world—Poles, Czechs, Slovaks and Serbs—who had lived for so long under foreign rule, their own country. Poland was created from the Polish-speaking parts of Russia and Germany, and by other treaties Czechoslovakia and Yugoslavia were formed from land formerly belonging to Austria and Hungary. The vast majority of the inhabitants of these 'new' countries were Poles or Czechs or Slovaks or Serbs as the case might be, but as for the sake of convenience and defence the frontiers of the

states had to follow as far as possible a river or a range of mountains, sometimes a small number of German-speaking people had to be included. It was impossible, for example, to make sure that every person living in Czechoslovakia was a Czech or a Slovak, and these 'minority' groups of Germans disliked being under the rule of another government which spoke a different language and had different customs. They did not think that the Czechs and the Poles had been in an even worse plight for a much longer time. A few years later, the German government, after the Nazis had come to power, accused the Polish and Czech governments of ill-treating the German inhabitants, and made this an excuse for taking back part of the land they had lost. This was one of the main causes of World War 2.

The new countries of Europe

Note how the new countries formed a barrier between the U.S.S.R. and Western Europe

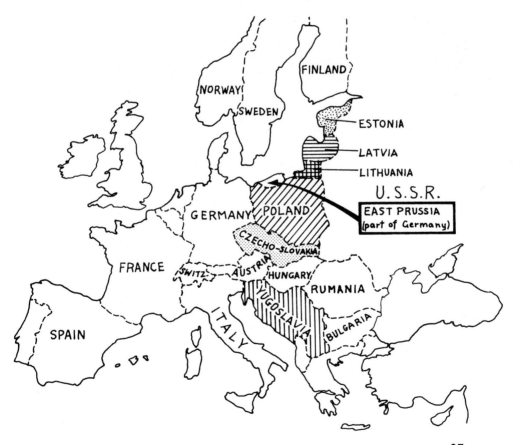

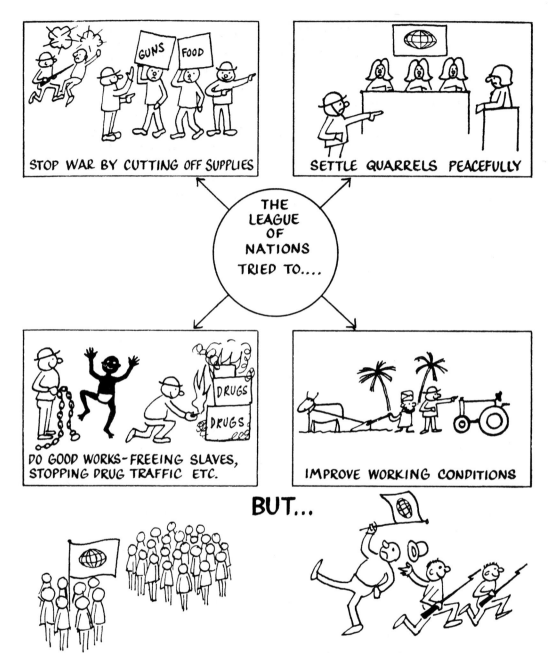

The Treaty of Versailles made the Germans very angry, especially as they had no representatives at the conference. Later on they argued that they had never agreed to the conditions and as the treaty had been forced on them, they need not obey it. Nevertheless, the men who drew it up thought they had done a very good job indeed and had made sure there would be peace in Europe for a very long time. They could not see at the time that the treaty was to be one of the causes of an even worse world war.

One very good idea did, however, come from the conference. The statesmen were determined to try to stop war for ever. Led by President Wilson they set up a kind of international club called the League of Nations with its headquarters in Geneva. About forty countries joined immediately, and it was hoped that if one member country had a quarrel with another, instead of going to war, both would send representatives to the League to try to settle the quarrel peacefully by discussion. If one nation did declare war on another all member nations would be urged to stop trading with the invading country until lack of supplies should bring fighting to an end.

Although its main aim was to maintain peace, the League tried to help in many other ways. It had an international court to which nations could bring shipping, fishing and other disputes for settlement; it did good work in freeing slaves, in stopping much of the drug traffic in opium, and in improving working conditions in less advanced countries.

Unfortunately, fewer than half the countries in the world belonged to the League. Russia did not join until 1934, America—one of the most powerful countries in the world—was not a member, while others came determined to upset it. The League had no army to enforce its decisions, so that any nation wishing to defy it could do so without fear. However, for a few years the League seemed to be working well, and did indeed, stop a few small wars. In the end it became obvious that the countries were too selfish and the most important part of the League's work—keeping peace—failed.

---

1. Who were the men who made the real decisions at the conference of Versailles? Why do you think these men claimed the right to do so?
2. What annoyed Germany most about the conference?
3. Do you think it was wrong to refuse to allow anyone to put Germany's case to the conference? (Think of what happens in a court of law, even if the prisoner pleads guilty.)
4. Why was Germany unable to pay the large sum demanded?
5. Why were the members of the conference anxious to make a string of 'new' countries from north to south across Europe?
6. What difficulties are likely to arise if a 'new' country is made by taking away and joining up parts of existing countries?

7. What were the ideas behind the creation of the new states of Czecho-slovakia and Yugoslavia, and the re-creation of Poland?
8. The map of the north-eastern corner of France (page 30) shows the frontier with Germany. It shows the two 'counties' of Alsace and Lorraine which Germany took from France in 1870, so that in 1914 the boundary between the two countries ran along the line marked with crosses. Noting particularly the deep, wide river Rhine, why do you think the French were especially anxious to have these two 'counties' back again?
9. What was the main purpose of the League of Nations?
10. How did the League try to stop wars?
11. Why did the League fail in its main task?
12. What is the name of the present organisation similar to the League?
13. Which parts of the Treaty of Versailles most upset countries and laid the foundation of another world war?
14. Encyclopaedia work:

   (a) What happened to the colonies which were taken from Germany? (Look under the word 'mandate' in an encyclopaedia.)
   (b) Until 1920 Turkey was a very underdeveloped country, and as one of Germany's defeated allies, she had her colonies taken away. One of Turkey's generals, Mustapha Kemal (Kemal Attaturk) set about bringing Turkey up to date after the war. Find out all you can about him, especially what he did in the matter of Turkish dress, the Turkish language and the position of Turkish women.

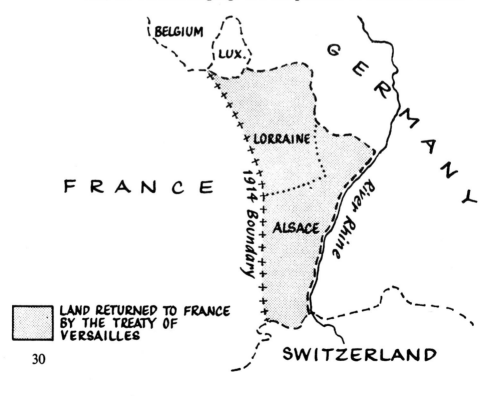

5

SOCIAL EFFECTS
OF WORLD WAR 1

Wars are always horrible, but like bombs which as well as killing human beings, knock down disease-ridden slums which should have been destroyed years earlier, some good can come from them. So it was with World War 1.

No good could possibly come from the death of at least ten million men, of course, nor from the billions of pounds' worth of damage that was caused. No one liked the very high taxes that had to be paid afterwards to pay for the war, and in Britain there was much unemployment and misery because countries such as Japan, which had not taken much part in the actual fighting or arms production, had taken over much of the world's trade. British firms found it difficult to sell their goods abroad, and as a result many had to close down or dismiss workers. In 1921, one man in six was out of work, and worse was to follow. The prices of most goods had risen sharply during the war; the cost-of-living index (that is roughly the

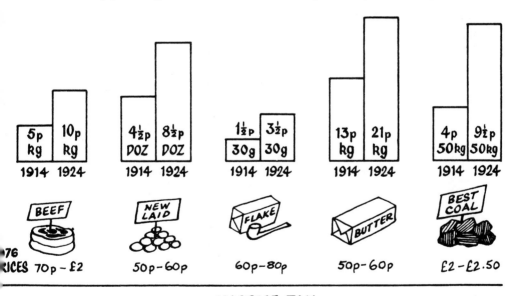

price of most essential goods and services) went up two and a half times between 1914 and 1920. It fell back a little in the mid-1920s but never again dropped to pre-war levels.

The miners in particular suffered badly as their wages were already below the average. In 1921 the government had to cut its spending. The coal mines which had been controlled by the government during the war were handed back to their private owners, who immediately announced their intention of cutting wages and increasing hours. This resulted in a strike which lasted three months. In 1925 a committee was appointed by the Conservative government to investigate the industry, and this advised that the miners' wages should be *reduced* and the hours *increased*. This was too much for the miners, who came out on strike. The leaders of the Trade Unions then told the government that unless it gave way over the mines, they would call a General Strike—that is, every major industry would close down. The government refused and, on May 4th 1926, factories, docks, powerstations and all industry stopped: trams, buses and trains ceased running, and no newspapers were printed. The whole country was at a standstill.

The only news was that sent out by the BBC, which had recently begun broadcasting, a single sheet government newspaper organised by Mr. Churchill and a TUC broadsheet. Thousands of volunteers drove buses and trains and unloaded ships. Nine days later everyone except the miners went back to work. The government then passed a law which made any strike that was general or sympathetic illegal. The Trade Unions and the Labour Party were very bitter about this Act which was repealed in 1946.

But there were some good results from the four terrible years of slaughter and destruction. Women, who before the war had been considered suitable only for running a home, had shown during the fighting that they were as useful as men by working in factories and on farms, driving buses and ambulances, acting as policemen and postmen, and even in more important jobs such as running businesses, offices and government departments. Having tasted this freedom, the women were determined not to return to the old way of life, and in 1918, partly as a reward for their good work and partly because they had shown themselves to be responsible citizens, women over 30 were given the right to vote.

The position of women
One of the most remarkable changes between 1914 and 1924 was in the position of women. In 1914 Britain was a man's country: women had almost no rights at all and their place was thought to be in the home. By 1924, largely because of the way they had worked during the war, women were almost equal to men.

This was only a beginning: in the years that followed more and more

1913
WOMEN SENT TO PRISON
FOR DEMANDING
THE VOTE

1918
VOTES FOR
WOMEN
OVER 30

1919
WOMEN ALLOWED
TO BE
LAWYERS

1923
8 WOMEN M.P.s

1912 – 1914   1924

jobs became open to women. They could, for example, now become lawyers and important civil servants. In the matter of dress too, they reacted
against the over-dressed, fussy and clumsy styles they had worn before the
war, and adopted much simpler and more sensible clothing. They smoked
and drank openly, drove motor cars, took part in energetic sports and
did many things that few of them would have dared to do ten years earlier.

During the actual fighting, men of all classes had stood side by side,
sharing the same dangers, the same hopes and the same dreadful way of
life. The humblest workman in the trenches found that the noblest nobleman was a man much like himself, with the same thoughts and the same
feelings as himself. Now that they were wearing the same clothes and doing
the same job, perhaps the only difference between them was the way in
which they spoke, and when the fighting had ended the poor labourer
could never feel the same way about the upper classes as he had done before the war. What was good enough for war was good enough for peace,
and the ordinary soldier had fought for a better way of life for everyone,

not only for the 'gentleman'. So, many of the barriers between the classes began to crumble as men streamed out of the army and back to civilian life.

In wartime, no money or effort is spared in developing inventions which will help to defeat the enemy. In particular, cars and aeroplanes were improved remarkably between 1914 and 1918. When peace returned the motor car was no longer an expensive, unreliable toy, and aeroplanes were bigger, faster and above all, safer. The factories which had been making vehicles for army use had developed mass production, and now switched over to cars and lorries and motor cycles for civilian use. Although cars were cheaper than they had been, they were still too expen-

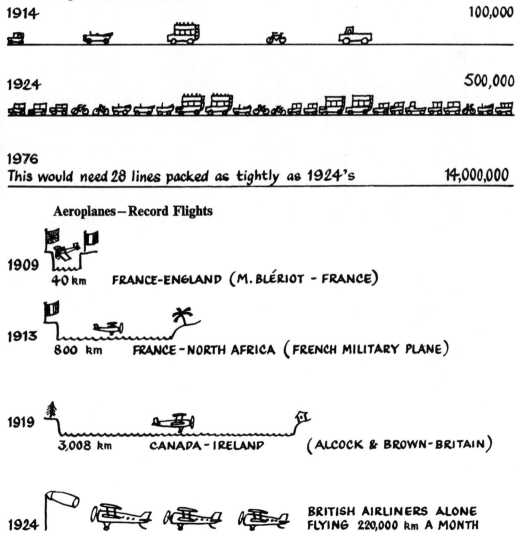

Transport – Motor vehicles

1914   100,000

1924   500,000

1976
This would need 28 lines packed as tightly as 1924's   14,000,000

Aeroplanes – Record Flights

1909
40 km   FRANCE-ENGLAND (M. BLÉRIOT - FRANCE)

1913
800 km   FRANCE - NORTH AFRICA (FRENCH MILITARY PLANE)

1919
3,008 km   CANADA - IRELAND   (ALCOCK & BROWN - BRITAIN)

1924   BRITISH AIRLINERS ALONE
            FLYING 220,000 km A MONTH

sive for ordinary working people to buy, but there were many more buses and coaches which enabled people to travel to work and on holiday at low rates. The working class were now beginning to be able to move about almost as freely as the upper classes could.

Aeroplanes had been developed perhaps even more than cars during the war, especially the large, heavy bombing planes, and after 1919 it was fairly easy to adapt these for passenger carrying. Slowly and hesitantly the first air services began, first to Europe, and then further and further afield. In 1909 an astounded nation could scarcely believe that a Frenchman, M. Blériot, had actually flown across the English Channel, a distance of less than 40 kilometres. It seemed a miracle: ten years later, two Englishmen, Alcock and Brown staggered the world by crossing the Atlantic in a bomber non-stop. The world of travel as we know it was being born.

Entertainments

Wireless was another of the scientific 'toys' which was developed rapidly during the war, and in 1922 it was considered sufficiently advanced for a public broadcasting system to be opened. The B.B.C. was formed by six companies which made electrical and radio apparatus, and transmissions began. The sets were very crude, few people had them, and those who did usually made them themselves. There were only a few hours of broadcasting each day, and most of the programmes were very serious. This is a typical day's transmission.

3.30–4.0 The Wireless Trio, with soprano solos. (Close down)
5.0 –5.30 Talks: (a) Colour Schemes.
                (b) For those who want to write. (Close down)
7.0 News, followed by gardening talk and the Grenadier Guards Band. (close down)
9.10 Talk by the editor of *The Wireless World* entitled 'Aerials and Earths.'
9.45 Dance music.

The cinema was popular with seats from 1½p to 6p generally. Some expensive cinemas charged as much as 11½p for the best seats. The films until 1927 were, of course, silent, and the most popular were serials and Charlie Chaplin comedies.

Before the cinema the young man might like to take his girl friend to a meal. Here are two bills of 1924 from a typical London café.

Stewed steak and carrots	4p	Soup	1p
Mashed potatoes	1p	Steak pie	3½p
Boiled raisin pudding	1p	Cabbage	1p
Coffee	1p	Roast potatoes	1½p
	7p	Trifle, custard	1½p
		Coffee	1p
			9½p

Gramophones had become popular too: these were clockwork-driven, with large funnel-shaped horns and needles that had to be changed after every side. Records of the new American music called 'ragtime' or 'jazz' cost about 10p and each side of a 25½ cm disc played for only two to three minutes.

---

1. The prices of most goods doubled approximately between 1914 and 1924. If they had gone on doubling every ten years from 1924 to 1974, what would the prices be now? e.g.,

	1914	1924	1934	1944	1954	1964	1974
Eggs:	2½p	5p	10p	20p	40p	80p	£1·20 a dozen

   Work out each item on the menus opposite and in the clothing list on p. 10, and see how it compares with today's prices.
2. Why do you think the prices of goods increased so much?
3. Why were taxes so high in 1924?
4. What signs were there that women were being given more freedom after the war? Give your answer under two headings—(a) freedom in political and public life, and (b) freedom in their private lives.
5. Which do you think was the most important freedom that women gained?
6. What effect did the war have on the feelings of the ordinary people towards the 'upper' classes? Why was this?
7. Why, in the war of 1914–1918, should cars, aeroplanes and radio have developed so rapidly?
8. What is a General Strike? What did the trade unions hope to do in the General Strike of 1926? How did the Government prevent a repetition of this strike?
9. Work out how many people there were, on average, to each car in the years 1914, 1924, 1964.

   1914 population 42,000,000. Number of cars,   100,000
   1924 population 44,000,000 Number of cars,   500,000
   1964 population 53,000,000. Number of cars, 10,000,000
   What do you think these figures indicate?

10. What changes took place in the field of entertainment after the war?
11. Find out from a local café what the meals listed on page 36 would cost today.
12. Encyclopaedia work:
    (a) What is the standard rate of income tax for this year?
    (b) What do the letters BBC stand for NOW? What did they stand for in 1922 when the BBC began?

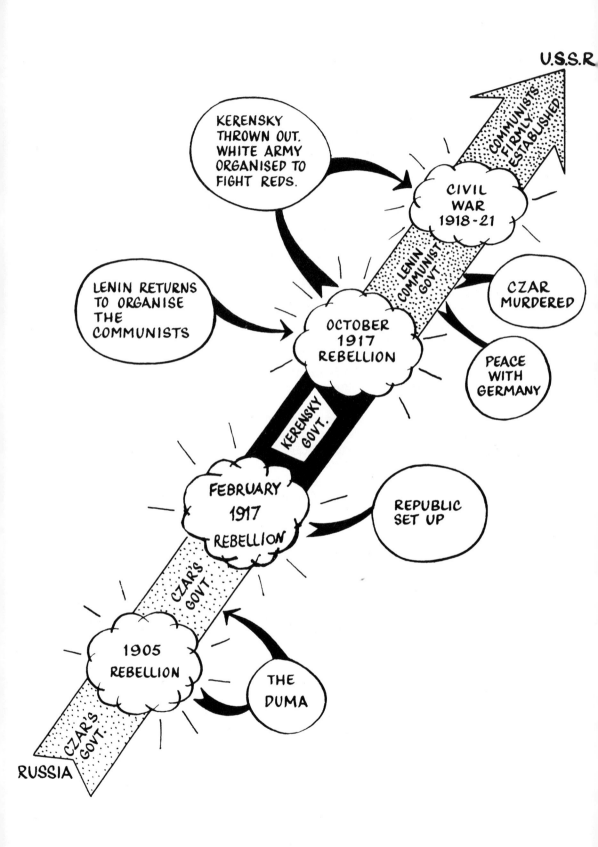

6

COMMUNISM AND THE RUSSIAN REVOLUTION OF 1917

The political belief called communism began with a Jewish lawyer named Karl Marx who was forced to flee to London from his native Germany in 1849 for supporting the working people against their masters. In 1867 he wrote a book called *Das Kapital* (Capital) in which he said that the capitalists —that is, the rich owners of factories, lands and shops—were treating the working class like slaves, and making bigger and bigger fortunes for themselves from the workers' efforts. Marx went on to say that the capitalists would go on growing richer and richer, and that the working class would become poorer and poorer until there was a war between the two classes. The poor, Marx said, would win this struggle: they would take over control of all industry, land and commerce, and would enjoy the profits for themselves. The workers would even govern the country one day, Marx continued, but at the time this seemed impossible. The destruction of the aristocracy, the rise of the working class and the ownership of all industry and land by the state is the essence of modern communism, which tends to be strongest in underdeveloped countries where the workers are desperately poor and oppressed by the ruling class. Naturally, the poorer the people, the more they long for the luxuries they see the rich enjoying, and they look to communism to give them what they consider a fairer share of the good things of life.

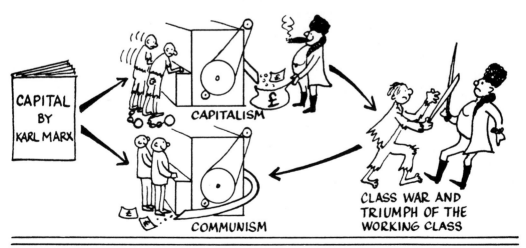

CAPITAL BY KARL MARX

CAPITALISM

COMMUNISM

CLASS WAR AND TRIUMPH OF THE WORKING CLASS

Before 1917 Russia was very poor and underdeveloped, and in many ways was more like a country of the middle ages.

The amount of coal and iron produced, the length of the railways and the value of exports each year gives a good idea of the state of development of a country in the early years of the twentieth century. Here are the figures for Britain, Germany, France and Russia for the years 1906–8. The figures for iron, coal and exports are given per head of the population, and the railways in metres for every square kilometre of territory. This gives a true picture of just how underdeveloped Russia was.

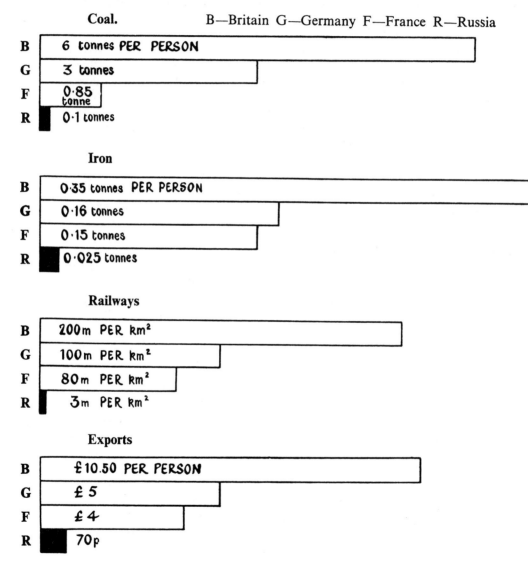

Coal.   B—Britain G—Germany F—France R—Russia

B | 6 tonnes PER PERSON
G | 3 tonnes
F | 0·85 tonne
R | 0·1 tonnes

Iron

B | 0·35 tonnes PER PERSON
G | 0·16 tonnes
F | 0·15 tonnes
R | 0·025 tonnes

Railways

B | 200m PER km²
G | 100m PER km²
F | 80m PER km²
R | 3m PER km²

Exports

B | £10.50 PER PERSON
G | £5
F | £4
R | 70p

To add to this, in Russia an average of 8 people in every 10 could neither read nor write: in Britain, Germany and France illiteracy had almost vanished.

All the power rested with the Czar, or king, backed by a small group of powerful nobles and the church. The majority of people were treated little better than animals, with never enough food, clothing or shelter. Much of the money they did earn was taken from them in the form of taxes by the greedy landowners, who lived in magnificent luxury. The government was weak and powerless when dealing with the nobles, but savage and cruel when dealing with the workers. For a very small offence a man could be sent to prison, or to exile in the mines of Siberia where often cold and appalling conditions put an end to his sufferings. The officials—police, tax collectors, judges—were as much tyrants as the nobles, and were usually corrupt and easily bribed. This is how Tolstoy, the famous Russian novelist describes an incident on the convict march to Siberia.

(The convicts—criminals, political prisoners and exiles, together with their women and children, have all been sent to Siberia. They are marched hundreds of kilometres through all weathers, chained together until they finally arrive at the prison. This incident occurs on the march.)

"The prisoners were counted, and the chains on their legs examined, and those who were to march in couples were linked together with manacles. But suddenly the angry authoritative voice of the officer shouting something was heard, and the sound of a blow as well as the crying of a child... The officer, a sturdy fellow with fair moustaches, frowning, and uttering words of coarse abuse, stood rubbing the palm of his right hand, which he had hurt by striking a prisoner in the face. Before him stood a tall thin convict with half his head shaven, and dressed in a cloak too short for him and trousers much too long, wiping a bleeding face with one hand and holding a shrieking little girl wrapped in a shawl with the other.

'I'll give it you (foul abuse). I'll teach you to argue. You're to give her to the women!' shouted the officer. 'Now then, on with them.'

The convict had been carrying his little daughter all the way from Tomsk, where his wife had died of typhus. The officer had now ordered him to be manacled. The exile's explanations that he could not carry the child if he were manacled irritated the officer, who happened to be in a bad temper, and he gave the troublesome prisoner a beating for not obeying at once...

The murmur among the prisoners grew louder. 'All the way from Tomsk they were not put on,' came a hoarse voice from someone in the rear ... 'Who's that?' shouted the officer, as if he had been stung, and rushed into the crowd. 'I'll teach you the law. Who spoke? You? You?' 'Everybody says so, because—' said a short, broad-faced prisoner. Before he had finished speaking the officer hit him in the face with both hands. 'Mutiny is it? I'll show you what mutiny means. I'll have you all shot like dogs, and the authorities will be only too thankful. Take the girl.'"

(*Resurrection*, by Leo Tolstoy)

There had been a minor revolution in 1905, and as a result the Czar had been forced to allow a parliament of sorts, called the Duma, to be elected. It had little power, however, and the Czar could over-rule any measures it passed. Having at last a parliament, only to find it completely useless, made the people more bitter than ever in their hatred of the ruling class.

So Russia struggled on, and in 1914 entered the war against Germany on behalf of her Serbian allies. By 1917 her armies had suffered dreadful losses and were close to defeat. The soldiers, brave though they were, could not hope to win with the old-fashioned weapons they were given and with the poor way in which they were led. While the men at the front were half-frozen, half-fed, and equipped often with only one rifle between every two or three men, the majority of the generals were enjoying themselves far from the war, safe, and making money in a dozen illegal ways.

By February 1917 the Russian people could stand it no longer. After a hard winter there was a desperate shortage of food, and many workers went on strike. The Czar sent soldiers to deal with the strikers, but a part of the army mutinied and joined them in their protest. Immediately the country was in an uproar: in the confusion the Czar and his family were seized and imprisoned. Alexander Kerensky, a member of the Duma, formed a government and declared Russia a republic. He wanted to continue the fight against Germany, but all that most Russians wanted was peace, so the confusion grew steadily.

Meanwhile the Germans smuggled into Russia one of Karl Marx's most devoted followers called Lenin. He had been exiled by the Czar because of his revolutionary ideas, and now he saw his job as organising the army, navy and workers into a communist army. While the rioting was at its height, Lenin and his communists, who were really the only organised party, stepped in and seized power. Kerensky's government was turned out, and a communist one under Lenin took its place. This was the October Revolution which the Russians celebrate every year.

Immediately the lands and homes of the nobles were seized, and many of the aristocrats were killed. When the soldiers on the battle front heard this, they mutinied, sometimes murdering their officers, and fled back to their homes. Lenin at once signed a peace treaty with the Germans which gave away vast areas of the country: for Russia the World War was over, but an even more bitter conflict was just beginning. In July 1918 the Czar was murdered. Kerensky failing to gather an army fled to England but terrible civil war began between those opposing Lenin (Whites) and the communists (Reds). By the time of the Whites' defeat in 1920 the whole of Russia was starving and on the point of complete collapse.

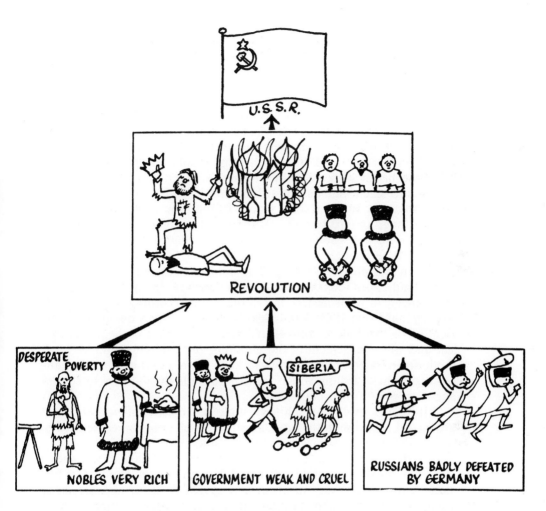

In a communist state, however, everything belongs to the people, so the peasants and workers, who were no longer toiling for a nobleman's profit but for their own good, threw themselves into the almost impossible task of rebuilding their shattered and ruined country. In 1922, four of the separate Russian communist countries joined together under the leadership of Lenin to form the Union of Soviet Socialist Republics. The U.S.S.R. which was to become such a powerful influence on the history of the world had been born.

Here are some short extracts from Marx's book *Das Kapital*. This is a picture of the industrial parts of England about a hundred years ago. Marx claims that these evils are caused by the greedy factory owners squeezing their workpeople in order to make more profits. It is on this sort of evidence that Marx says that capitalism must be abolished and that the workers themselves must own the factories.

43

"In the notorious London district of Bethnal Green, every Monday and Tuesday morning, there is held an open market, in which children of both sexes at ages from nine years upwards hire themselves out to the London silk manufacturers. 'The usual terms are 1/8 (8½p) a week' (this belongs to the parents) and '2d (1p) for myself and tea'. The scene and language while this market is going on are quite disgraceful . . ."

"The first school we visited was kept by a Mrs. Ann Killin. Upon asking her to spell her name, she straightway made a mistake, by beginning with the letter C, but, correcting herself immediately, she said her name began with a K... her handwriting left no doubt as to her unfitness to teach. She herself also acknowledged she could not keep the register . . . In the second school I found the schoolroom 15 feet (4·5 m) long, and 10 feet (3 m) wide, and counted in this space 75 children, who were gabbling something unintelligible."

"It will be enough now therefore, to refer to one point—the terribly high mortality of working-class children in the first year of life... In England... per 100,000 children under one year living at any time... there are ... in Manchester, 26,125 (deaths). According to an official enquiry in the year 1861 ... the high mortality is mainly due to employment of mothers away from their homes, and to the consequent neglect and mismanagement of the children; to unsuitable food, lack of food, dosing with opiates (drugs to keep them quiet) etc.; also to an estrangement of feeling which sometimes leads the mothers to starve and even poison their children."

"It (that is, printing machines) employs two kinds of workers: one grown up ... the other, the boys, mostly from eleven to seventeen years of age...They perform this weary task, in London especially, for fourteen, fifteen, or sixteen hours at a stretch, during several days of the week, and often for thirty-six hours at a stretch, with only two hours rest for sleep and meals. Many of them are unable to read; and are, as a rule, little better than savages, quite abnormal creatures. Their wages, though rather high for boys, do not increase proportionately as they grow up, and the majority of then cannot look for advancement to the better paid post of machine minder... As soon as they get too old for boy's work, at the latest therefore when they are seventeen, they are discharged... to swell the ranks of the criminal classes."

"In the year 1865 there were 3,217 coalmines in Great Britain, and only 12 inspectors. A Yorkshire mine owner ... calculates that—quite apart from the fact that office work absorbs so much of the inspectors' time—it is only possible for each mine to be visited once every ten years. We hardly need wonder, therefore, there has been a steady increase in the number and severity of mining disasters, which sometimes lead to the sacrifice of from two to three hundred miners at once. Such are the beauties of 'free' capitalist production!"

Coco, the famous Russian-born clown of Bertram Mills' circus, was in an army hospital in Petrograd (now called Leningrad) in 1917 after being wounded in the war. As food was so short any soldier who could walk was given what clothing could be found and turned into the street. This is how Coco described the beginning of the Revolution in his autobiography.

"... I was turned loose in the snows of Petrograd.

But this was a Petrograd I did not know. The city was starving. Everywhere the workers were on strike. Hoardings carried posters warning them to stop their strike on pain of twenty-five years in Siberia— or the firing squad. There were muttering crowds, grey pinched faces, and wailing children. People, literally starving to death, huddled into the angles of the walls trying to keep off the deadly cold. The streets were thick with snow and ice. And everywhere armed police moved the miserable people on.

... As I stood there, shivering, a motor lorry came roaring down the street. It was packed with students, soldiers and sailors on leave, and a few women.

The lorry stopped in the middle of the crowd. A long-haired student stood up on a box and addressed the crowd in passionate language.

'My comrades!' he cried. 'The war is being lost. At home they are starving you to death. There is no hope for you! Are you going to stand by and see your husbands starved to death, your wives dying from the cold and your children trampled underfoot?'

As he finished his long speech, he whipped off the lorry a red cloth, which he waved like a banner. I saw then that the lorry was full of weapons—bayonets, swords, revolvers and ammunition.

The crowd seemed to go mad. What cries and cheers came from those poor weak throats..."

(The Government soldiers were ordered not to let the crowds cross the main bridge in the town to meet the crowds on the other side. Then Coco continues...)

"A tired old man, carrying a dinner-basin tied up in a red handkerchief tried to push his way through the crowd. A Cossack (soldier) stopped him. In a thin, piteous voice, the old man explained that if he could reach the other side of the river his daughter might let him have a little food. Looking sadly at him, the Cossack refused and turned away. The old man trailed wearily after him... This annoyed the Cossack officer. He ordered the soldier to take the old man away. The soldier did not move. With an angry oath the officer rode up to the old man and slashed him furiously across the face with his riding-whip. The old fellow dropped his empty basin and began to cry.

Without a word, the Cossack drew his sabre and killed the officer.

Pandemonium broke loose. The Cossacks killed all their officers.

45

The crowd went mad and tried to rush the bridge. But from every housetop along the quays there came a rain of bullets, fired by policemen hidden there with machine-guns. Many people were killed and the bodies tossed over into the river. A howling, impassioned mob streamed across the bridge and stormed the public buildings.

The revolution had begun."

(Coco the Clown, by N. Poliakoff)

THE FLAG OF THE U.S.S.R. (UNION OF SOVIET SOCIALIST REPUBLICS)

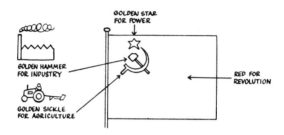

The flag of the new state tells the story of the country: after revolution (red background) the power (golden star) rests with the workers in industry (golden hammer) and agriculture (golden sickle).

---

1. Who founded communism and where did he set out its aims?
2. What are the three main aims of communism?
3. Where is communism most likely to succeed? Why do you think this is so?
4. What is the difference between the ownership of factories, shops, banks etc. in communist and capitalist countries?
5. Why were the vast mass of the Russian people ready to begin a revolution?
6. What was the Duma, and how successful was it for the people of Russia?
7. What caused the revolution to break out in Russia in 1917?
8. What part did Lenin play in the revolution?
9. Why were the communists able to seize power from the Kerensky government in October, 1917?
10. Who were the opposing sides in the Civil War, 1918–1920? Give the names of the leaders.
11. How does the flag of the U.S.S.R. tell the story of the success of the revolution of 1917?
12. Copy the chart on page 38 (Russian Governments 1900–1924).

13. Encyclopaedia work:

    (a) Where is Karl Marx buried?

    (b) What happened to Kerensky?

    (c) What was the name of the city we call Leningrad (Lenin's town in Russian) before 1924?

    (d) Who was Trotsky and what happened to him?

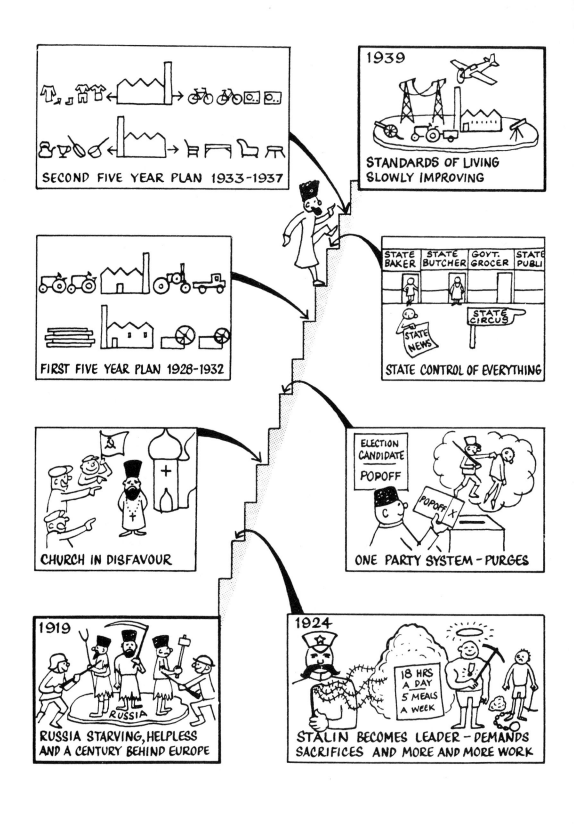

7

THE SOVIET CLIMB TO POWER 1919-1939

The story of the U.S.S.R. between 1919 and 1939 is almost like a fairy tale, and most of the incredible success is due to one man, Joseph Stalin whose energy, cruelty and ruthlessness turned Russia from an almost ruined wasteland to a mighty nation in twenty years. In 1919 Russia was a century behind most of Europe in many ways: she had little machinery, little trade and industrial methods were hopelessly out-of-date. Twenty years later she had leapt forward a hundred years with industry, communication and machinery which compared favourably with any but the most highly developed countries, such as the United States, Britain and Germany. But no country can move forward at such a rate without a great deal of suffering: so it was with Russia.

Lenin, the leader of the revolution, died soon after the civil war had ended after an assassin's bullet provoked a heart condition and a series of strokes, and was followed as dictator of Russia by Joseph Stalin. Cruel, cunning and completely without pity, Stalin saw that his country could not rest now that the revolution was over. In fact, the people must now work harder than ever before and manage with less and less food and fewer and fewer goods as the civil war had destroyed much that did exist. Life for the Russians was bitter indeed, with long hours of work; back-breaking labour with inefficient tools; little food, comfort or leisure. Sacrifice after sacrifice was demanded by the leaders to repair the shattered country and to ensure that the new communist state survived, for almost every country in the world would have liked to see it perish.

The Russian people already knew what hard work meant, for their former masters, the nobles, had driven them hard with threats of punishment: but now most of them worked willingly for they realised that in the end they were toiling for themselves. The only large group which did object were the wealthy peasant farmers, or Kulaks, for whom the new way of life seemed worse than their old one. Rather than hand over their farms to the government collective scheme they slaughtered their cattle and burnt the crops. As a punishment, and a warning, it is thought that over a million were sent to labour camps or executed. Stalin knew that if one small group succeeded in defying the government, the rest might follow, and the whole communist system might collapse.

The Church in Russia was immensely powerful, and was often as corrupt as the nobles had been. Stalin saw that its influence must be checked as it was no friend of the communist party. He did not outlaw religion, as this would have offended many people, for the Russians are very devout, but he carried on a campaign against the church by mocking the priests, turning many of their buildings into museums and discouraging younger people from attending services. Later on, when the communist government felt more secure, this attitude was relaxed a little.

Stalin saw that if the country was to be driven to success there could be no arguing in the Supreme Soviet, or parliament, so all parties except the communists were banned. There were elections, but the voting papers contained a single list of names, all communists, and the voters had to indicate whether they approved of the list or not. Anyone who opposed the party in any way—and thousands who were perfectly innocent and whose only crime was that they had made an enemy of a party official—was ruthlessly hunted down by the OGPU (later the NKVD), the secret police, and imprisoned or murdered. Millions, perhaps, whose only crime was that Stalin thought they might grow popular enough to compete with him, were killed in the great Purges, which are the greatest blot on Stalin's career.

1921

700,000 MEMBERS   175,000 EXPELLED, MANY EXECUTED

1928

1,300,000 MEMBERS   250,000 FOLLOWERS OF TROTSKY
EXPELLED

1933

3,500,000 MEMBERS   800,000 EXPELLED

No one knows how many people were executed in the Great Purge of 1934–38 which followed. Estimates vary from 1,000,000 to 10,000,000. Perhaps similar numbers went to labour camps. Party and non-party members were killed indiscriminately. The higher ranks of the Red Army

50

suffered particularly badly and when the war came the loss of the experienced senior officers was felt badly.

In a communist country, of course, there can be no large-scale private trading or industry, as the owner would become rich at the expense of his employees, so the Soviet government took over all business. There were state railways, state banks, state factories, state shops, state newspapers and state farms. Even the few entertainments were controlled by the government—state cinemas, state opera and ballet, state theatres, state orchestras and state circuses. Small, one-man businesses such as peasants selling their surplus produce, were, however—and still are—allowed.

Progress in building the U.S.S.R. into a modern state was slow until the first Five Year Plan was drawn up in 1928. Everything was now planned by the government for a great advance in industry and agriculture. Everyone toiled at the job he or she had been given—for men and women worked side by side in all tasks—and the newly built factories began turning out tractors, lorries, heavy machines, railways, hydro-electric power plants and other basic manufacturing equipment in a steady stream, which grew as the years passed. Some people, who had been expecting comforts and luxuries from the factories, were disappointed, but it was obvious that the vital machinery must come first. By 1933 the industry and agriculture of the U.S.S.R. were turning out more than they had ever done in history.

Immediately the first Five Year Plan ended, a second was organised, and this time there was a little time for the people who had worked so hard to relax. Goods which helped to make life easier—clothing, shoes, radios, household goods, furniture and houses themselves—began to roll from the factories and machinery built in the first Five Year plan, though heavy industrial machinery and transport was still the most important item. Vast new industrial cities began to appear all over the vast country, and the great movement from the country to the towns began.

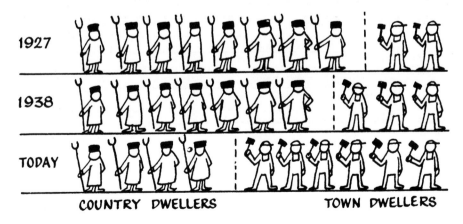

COUNTRY DWELLERS   TOWN DWELLERS

The changes in production in Russia because of the Five Year plans (1928–1938).

The first figure is the production in 1928, the second after 1938.

1928	AFTER 1938	1928	AFTER 1938
OIL		GRAIN	
11 m. TONNES A YEAR	31 m. TONNES A YEAR	20 m. TONNES A YEAR	40 m. TONNES A YEAR
COAL		TRACTORS	
30 m. TONNES A YEAR	150 m. TONNES A YEAR	1300 A YEAR	32,000 A YEAR
STEEL		MACHINE TOOLS	
5 m. TONNES A YEAR	17 m. TONNES A YEAR	2,000 A YEAR	45,000 A YEAR

1928	RAILWAYS	77,000 km
AFTER 1938		97,000 km

1928	ROADS	26,000 km
AFTER 1938		88,500 km

52

1911	6,000,000 PUPILS	Ordinary schools
1927	11,000,000 PUPILS	
1936	30,000,000 PUPILS	
1971	40,000,000 PUPILS	

		Universities, Colleges
9	1911	
87	1927	
597	1936	
834	1973	

One of the most important of all the aspects of the Five Year Plans was the building of schools and colleges. Before the revolution about two persons in ten in Russia could read and write, and the communists realised that to make their country up-to-date and prosperous the people must be educated. Not only did they need highly-trained scientists and engineers to design and manufacture the new machinery, but also the ordinary workmen had to be literate to be able to use the complicated equipment. A man did not really need to be able to read to milk a cow or use a scythe, but he did to work a lathe or drive a train.

The chart shows how this educational programme was carried out. The number of children at school rose from 6 to 30 millions between 1911 and 1936, and even more remarkable, the nine universities of 1911 had expanded into almost six hundred twenty five years later. In addition, particularly in the 1920's and 1930's there were thousands of schools for adults who had never been fortunate enough to go to school. Here, after work, they could learn to read and write and also how to improve their skills.

By the end of the Second Five Year Plan in 1937, the Russians, with production soaring and education immeasurably improved, were much more comfortable, prosperous and powerful than they had ever been. The third Five Year Plan was begun, but unfortunately it was so obvious that war was coming that the factories, instead of turning out cars, refrigerators and other luxuries, had to turn to tanks, aeroplanes and guns, so that the consumer march forward was halted for over ten years.

---

1. What were Stalin's good points—and his bad ones?

2. Who were the Kulaks and why did they oppose the communist ideas? What happened to them?
3. Why was Stalin so severe with the Kulaks?
4. Why did Stalin attack the Russian Church? Why did he find it difficult to ban religion altogether, even though he was so powerful?
5. How did Stalin break the power of the church?
6. What kind of elections are held in Russia?
7. What is the Russian parliament called today?
8. Are all privately-owned businesses banned in Russia? Who does own the factories, shops and commerce?
9. What were the objects of the First Five Year Plan?
10. What difference was there between the first and second Five Year Plans?
11. What happened to the third Five Year Plan?
12. Why do you think there was a large movement of people from the country to the towns after 1927?
13. Of the items mentioned on page 52 (diagram of increase of production during the Five Year Plans) which ones showed the greatest increase between 1928–38? Why do you think the Russians concentrated on these?
14. Which products increased least in the years 1928–38?
15. Why did the Russians consider education such an important part of their Five Year Plans?
16. Why is there less need for adult schools to teach illiterates today in Russia than there was in the 1920s and 1930s?

8

THE RISE OF HITLER 1919-1934

A man who rules a country completely on his own without having to consult a parliament or the people is called a dictator. Between 1919 and 1939 a number of countries in Europe were ruled by dictators, and of these the most important were Adolf Hitler of Germany, Benito Mussolini of Italy and Joseph Stalin of the U.S.S.R.

After the war of 1914–1918 Germany was left in a dreadful condition. The country was almost bankrupt, there was not enough work, there was little food, and violence and riots broke out everywhere. Scores of men and political parties preached and raved that they alone had the secret for making Germany strong, powerful and rich again, and among these was a group of about twenty workmen in Munich who later called themselves the National Socialist German Workers' Party (NAZIS for short). In 1919, Hitler, who had been a corporal in the war and who was now a spy for the government, was sent to watch and report on the group as they met in a public house, for they were suspected of being communists.

After attending several of their meetings, Hitler was convinced that National Socialists had the right answer to all of Germany's problems. He joined the party and soon, because of his ability to speak so convincingly, became their leader. This is how he describes his entry into the party in his book:

> "When I returned to the barracks that night I was facing the most difficult problem of my life... should I join or refuse? I became convinced I must take the step. I declared myself ready to accept membership ... and received my certificate. I was numbered seven..."

At this stage the party funds were exactly 7·50 marks!

By 1923 the Nazi party had several hundred members, and Hitler attempted to overthrow the government of Bavaria by marching with his supporters on the parliament buildings in Munich. The police opened fire on the marchers, who quickly broke up and fled, leaving sixteen Nazis dead on the street. Hitler himself was arrested, charged with treason and thrown into prison. Although sentenced to five years he served only thirteen months, and those in comparative luxury. Most of the time he spent writing a book called *Mein Kampf* (My Struggle) which was to become the 'bible' of the Nazis. In the book, as well as explaining what a wonderful man he, Adolf

Hitler, was, he set out his plans for making Germany great once again. The main points were:

1. Germany had not been really beaten by the Allies in the war: she had been betrayed by Jews and communists who must therefore be utterly destroyed.
2. The Germans were the master race of the world: they must all be united under one leader and given whatever territory was needed for this.
3. The Treaty of Versailles was not binding on Germany as it had been forced on her (she had no representatives at the conference) and it need not be obeyed.

ALL GERMANS MUST BE UNITED UNDER ONE LEADER

MY STRUGGLE
A. HITLER

THE TREATY OF VERSAILLES WAS UNJUST AND MUST BE TORN UP

ALL JEWS AND COMMUNISTS MUST BE DESTROYED AS THEY ARE THE CAUSE OF ALL GERMANY'S TROUBLES

THE GERMANS ARE THE MASTER RACE AND MUST HAVE WHAT THEY WANT

In 1924 Hitler was once more at liberty, and the Nazis were promising the German people what they wanted most—power, wealth and freedom. The condition of Germany was even more desperate than it had been a few years before, so that people were only too willing to try anything that offered some hope of improvement. Thousands joined the party which after 1920 used the infamous black swastika symbol. Hitler organised a large private army called the Storm Troopers, or SA, who, dressed in brown shirts and jackboots, were supposed to keep order at political meetings. A very small select group of the SA were Hitler's personal bodyguard, or SS. As the party grew larger and Hitler more powerful, the SA became more brutal and more ruthless, murdering indiscriminately anyone who opposed them. This is how Hitler describes the early SA men in *Mein Kampf* (My Struggle):

"When our political meetings first started I... organised a suitable defensive squad—a squad composed of young men. These young men had been brought up to realise that the best means of defence was attack. How those young men did their job! Like a swarm of hornets they tackled disturbers at our meetings, regardless of superiority of numbers, however great, indifferent to wounds and bloodshed ..."

This is what happened at one meeting when a rival party began to make trouble:

"In a few moments the hall was filled with a yelling shrieking mob. Numerous beer-mugs flew like howitzers (shells) above their heads. Amid this uproar one heard the crash of chair legs, the crashing of mugs, groans, yells and screams.

It was a mad spectacle. I stood where I was and could observe my boys doing their duty, every one of them..."

Between 1929 and 1933 many famous and wealthy Germans joined the Nazi party, and money poured into the funds. Some of this came from people who really believed in Hitler and his political ideas, but more from men who hoped to gain wealth and power from rearming Germany. At the elections of 1930 (Germany still had a properly-elected parliament at this time) over a hundred Nazi MPs were returned, making the National Socialists the second largest party. This was largely because Germany's plight was now worse than in 1924. The collapse of world trade left many of her factories idle and millions of unemployed men were ready to vote for any party that promised an improvement. Three years later, after much political trouble, the President, old General von Hindenburg, made Hitler Chancellor. In 1934, when Hindenburg died, Hitler made himself President as well as Chancellor. Other political parties were eliminated, and Hitler had almost complete power: all he had to do was to get rid of anyone who still opposed him or threatened his position. First on the list was the SA, which

under Rohm was a powerful force. In July 1934 Rohm and other chief officers were murdered on Hitler's orders, and its influence destroyed. From its most fanatical members he built up the SS to 100,000 men, all absolutely dedicated to himself. The SS included not only Hitler's bodyguard but, more important, the Gestapo (the dreaded secret police) and the men who ran and guarded the concentration camps.

The Gestapo had spies everywhere—in schools, factories and even private houses—and they reported anyone criticising Hitler or the Nazi party. Children were trained to betray their friends, teachers, and even parents, and once betrayed, the SS men stepped in to arrest them. From arrest, it was a very short step to execution: on one night alone, 30th June, 1934, hundreds of Hitler's old Nazi friends were murdered on his orders as he thought that they might oppose some of his more violent plans.

The Jews in particular were persecuted as Hitler had promised in *Mein Kampf*. At first they were jeered at, humiliated and made to wear placards whenever they went out in the streets bearing such words as 'I am a filthy Jew'. Later, their rights as citizens were taken away—for example, they were not allowed in certain shops, or entertainments, nor allowed to become lawyers or doctors. Finally they were rounded up and thrown into prisons. A fortunate few managed to escape to Britain, France, America, and other countries, but the vast majority were herded like animals into the slave labour and concentration camps, where they were brutally treated, starved, tortured and slaughtered in thousands.

The *Annual Register* (1938), an annual record of world events of the year, describes what happened when a German was killed in Paris by a Jew:

"In Berlin wrecking squads tore through the town at 2 a.m. setting fire to synagogues and to Jewish shops... Other squads under the supervision of men in Storm Troopers' (SA) uniform, and armed with hammers and axes, broken open the homes of Jews and smashed furniture and everything else they could lay hands on. In provincial towns, not only were the homes destroyed with savage brutality, but the families chased into the streets. The number of victims who suffered death will probably never be known. Nor will the number of suicides among Jews be established. Whole families took their own lives in order to escape the attack of the hooligans. Those who remained were hunted like animals, arrested and taken to concentration camps.

And the German authorities? On November 13th Herr Goering (a leading Nazi)... ordered Jews to make good at their own expense the damage which had been done by the SA hooligans to their shops and houses. Insurance claims of German Jews were to be paid over to the German government. To crown all, a fine of 1,000,000,000 marks was imposed on the Jews in Germany for the murder of Herr vom Rath ..."

All this did not take place in the middle ages, but in the lifetime of your grandparents.

The Nazis paid great attention to the education of young people, and had them brought up in such a way as to make them tough, warlike and fanatical members of the party. Hitler describes the type of education a young German should have:

> "The People's State must organise its educational work in such a way that the bodies of the young will be ... trained from infancy onwards, so as to be tempered and hardened for the demands made on them in later years.
>
> The People's State ought to allow much more time for physical training in the school. It is nonsense to burden young brains with a load of material of which they will retain only a small part. Not a day should be allowed to pass in which the young pupil does not have one hour of physical training in the morning and one in the evening: every kind of sport and gymnastics should be included ... especially... boxing..."

Children were supposed to go back for physical training and toughening drill in their own time in the evening. Even after they had left school there was compulsory drill and training classes. Hitler also talked about girls' education. In order for Germany to have a large army in later years he said that girls should marry young and have many children. Their education was to be directed to this end:

> "Special importance (in girls' education) must be given to physical training, and only after that must the importance of ... mental training be taken into account. In the education of a girl the final goal always to be kept in mind is that she is one day to be a mother ..."

So, by one method or another, in a very short time everyone who opposed the Nazis was either dead or in one of the most terrible prisons in the world, the concentration camps. His followers were kept happy with great meetings, displays of military power, wild patriotic songs and wilder promises of the greatness of Germany. Now Hitler was complete master of his country, and almost the whole nation was hypnotised by his ravings and propaganda into believing in him.

---

1. Why do you think Germany was in such a terrible condition after the war? What had made her bankrupt? Why were the German people so angry and discontented? (For some reasons look back to Chapter 4—The Treaty of Versailles.)
2. What tells you just how small and powerless the National Socialist German Workers' party was when Hitler joined it? Why was Hitler soon made its leader?

3. What, in Hitler's book *Mein Kampf*, do you think pleased many Germans?
4. Who were the SA men and what was their purpose?
5. People joined the Nazi party for different reasons. Give some of these reasons and name the kind of person who would have joined for each.
6. How did the Nazi party manage to become the second largest party in the German parliament?
7. At what point do you think Hitler became really the master and dictator of Germany?
8. What was the Gestapo, and what was its duty in Hitler's Germany?
9. Why did Hitler turn on many of his oldest Nazi friends and have them murdered?
10. Describe some of the brutal measures the Nazis took against the Jews. Why did they do this?
11. What were the main ideas behind Hitler's plans for education in Germany?
12. Encyclopaedia work:
    (a) On page 55 three dictators are mentioned. All three are now dead. Find out what happened to each of them.
    (b) Find out all you can about these leading members of the Nazi party: Herman Goering, Josef Goebbels, Heinrich Himmler, Ribbentrop, Rudolf Hess.

9

LIFE IN THE THIRTIES

The 1930's fall into three parts: for the first three years Britain, like most of the rest of the world, was suffering from a terrible trade depression which brought mass unemployment and poverty. Then came a steady improvement at home with more work and increasing prosperity, but these better conditions were, for the last two years, overshadowed by the threat of World War 2 which hung like a black cloud over Europe.

After World War 1 factories and shops were busy making and selling goods which people had had to manage without during the war, though Europe had lost much of its overseas trade to such countries as Japan. In Britain, too, much of the machinery in the mines and factories was old-fashioned and inefficient which meant that British goods were often more expensive than those of some other countries. As a result many factories were working at only half speed and men were dismissed. This together with the mass demobilisation of all the wartime service men led to severe unemployment. By the end of 1921 over two million men could not find jobs. Although the number out of work dropped a little in the next six years, it never fell below one million and all the time Britain's trade position grew worse.

Prices were forced lower and lower by foreign competition until the manufacturers were losing money. More factories closed or reduced the number of their employees and the whole process began to build up: the more men out of work, the fewer goods were bought, which meant less work for the factories which in turn meant more unemployment.

The final disaster came in 1929 when America found herself in serious financial trouble. The price of shares on the New York Stock Exchange (Wall Street) fell so severely that thousands of banks and businesses went bankrupt. There was mass unemployment and poverty. Because the United States had been lending money to so many other countries and now had to reduce these loans, world trade dropped to less than half the figure it had been a few years earlier. In Britain the effect was immediate and terrible: hundreds of factories, especially in Scotland, Northern Ireland, South Wales, Lancashire, Northeast and Northwest England were forced to close.

By mid-1931 more than two and a half million people were out of work and worse was to follow. In January, 1932, there were three million unemployed—almost one-fifth of the whole working population. To make

Some of the causes of the depression 1929–33.

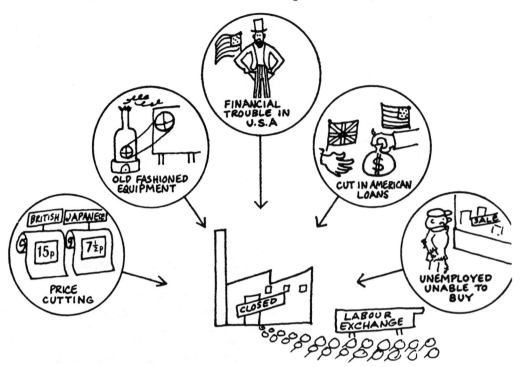

matters even worse in the most badly affected areas, many of the factories which were still producing goods moved to new premises nearer to London leaving behind them yet more unemployed. In the early thirties there were often long columns of dusty, hungry men marching towards the capital to

AVERAGE WEEKLY WAGES IN THE 1930'S			
BRICK LAYER	FARM WORKER	ENGINEER	MAN ON THE DOLE
£	£	£	£
3·50	1·50	3·00	0·85 ✳

✳ with wife and 3 children £1.46

demand that the government did something for them, preferably, find them work.

The men did, of course, receive a small amount of unemployment pay each week (the dole) from the government, but at 85p a week for a single man or £1.46 for a married man with three children, this was not enough to live on. In any case, the men wanted work, not charity.

Giving dole to over two million unemployed men each week soon left the government itself in a difficult position for money, and when it tried to borrow more from the United States the Americans refused unless the government reduced its own spending (1931). Immediately the pay of soldiers, sailors, policemen, teachers, civil servants and many others was cut; part of the Navy mutinied and refused to take the ships to sea. The position was desperate. To reduce still further its spending the government ordered that all unemployed men, after their unemployment pay had been exhausted had to take a 'Means test' which meant that they had to declare if they had any savings or if they had any more fortunate relative to help support them. If they had either, they could get no help from the government until these sources had all been used up.

To help reduce the number of men out of work the government and town councils began a number of public works, such as clearing slums, building roads and large estates of 'council' houses. These were houses

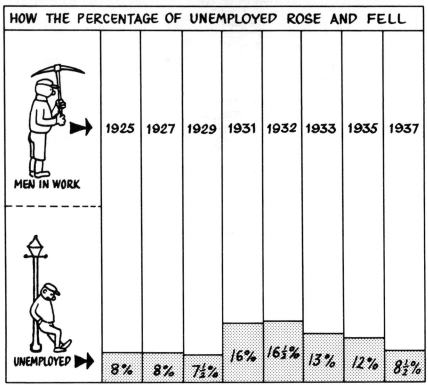

HOW THE PERCENTAGE OF UNEMPLOYED ROSE AND FELL

| | 1925 | 1927 | 1929 | 1931 | 1932 | 1933 | 1935 | 1937 |

MEN IN WORK

UNEMPLOYED

| 8% | 8% | 7½% | 16% | 16⅔% | 13% | 12% | 8½% |

owned by the local council, and let at reduced rents to people who needed them.

After 1933, however, the situation began to improve a little. The number of unemployed began slowly to fall and more goods were sold abroad.

Though conditions grew better at home, however, news from abroad was ominous. In 1934 Hitler defied the Treaty of Versailles and began rearming Germany: in 1935 Italy invaded and seized the backward state of Abyssinia, despite the Leage of Nations' protest, and in 1936 a bitter civil war broke out in Spain. Germany and Italy helped the rebels, who were led by General Franco, and Russia helped the government, which was eventually defeated.

Yet at first these troubles seemed to help at home, for the British government realised the danger of war and began to build warships, tanks, aeroplanes and other military equipment. This meant more factories, more work and higher wages for the majority, but in spite of all this, right until 1939 there were over a million unemployed who lived in poverty.

Throughout the 1930's the price of most goods remained fairly steady or fell slightly, but wages rose, so that most people who were employed found they could afford more luxuries.

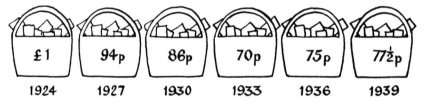

| £1 | 94p | 86p | 70p | 75p | 77½p |
| 1924 | 1927 | 1930 | 1933 | 1936 | 1939 |

How the price of the same basket of ordinary groceries changed.

There was a great demand for labour saving equipment as servants were now very difficult to obtain. Electric fires, electric irons, vacuum cleaners and gas equipment were very popular, and electric power spread from the large towns to country districts on great steel pylons. The consumption of electric power naturally rose very sharply.

There was more money for leisure, and as many more people now had paid holidays, a week or fortnight at the seaside, or even abroad, became common. The annual trip to the coast was made much easier by the introduction of a completely new idea, the holiday camp, which was begun in Britain as a commercial venture by Mr. Butlin. For the rest of the year the cinema was the main entertainment, and every week millions of people streamed into the huge new picture palaces that sprang up everywhere. To cope with the numbers, many cinemas in large towns began at eleven in the morning and ran continuously until midnight or even later. For home entertainment there was the gramophone and, of course, the radio, which was now found in almost every home. If one found the BBC programmes too serious, as many did, there were non-stop popular music sessions in English,

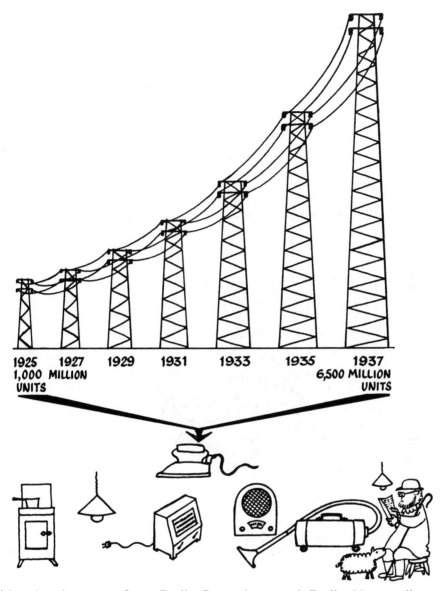

1925	1927	1929	1931	1933	1935	1937

1,000 MILLION
UNITS

6,500 MILLION
UNITS

with advertisements, from Radio Luxemburg and Radio Normandie. A good new bicycle cost about £3, and, best of all, a new Ford car could be bought for £100, especially if one had managed to win on the latest craze, football pools.

Cheap cars and cheap petrol brought motoring within the reach of thousands of working people for the first time, and the number of vehicles on the road more than doubled between 1927 and 1937. Unfortunately the number of accidents and deaths on the road rose sharply too, for both the roads and many of the people were still in the horse-and-cart days. Even today, with five or six times as many cars on the roads as in 1937, the

Changes in traffic and number of deaths on the road.

⊏⊐ 𝍏 = 100,000 CARS OR CARTS ⚰ = 1,000 DEATHS

Year	Cars	Carts	Deaths
1923	⊏⊐ ⊏⊐ ⊏⊐ ⊏⊐	𝍏 𝍏	⚰ ⚰ ⚰
1927	⊏⊐ ⊏⊐ ⊏⊐ ⊏⊐ ⊏⊐ ⊏⊐ ⊏⊐ ⊏⊐	𝍏	⚰ ⚰ ⚰ ⚰ ⚰
1931	⊏⊐ ⊏⊐ ⊏⊐ ⊏⊐ ⊏⊐ ⊏⊐ ⊏⊐ ⊏⊐ ⊏⊐ ⊏⊐	𝍏	⚰ ⚰ ⚰ ⚰ ⚰ ⚰
1934	⊏⊐ ⊏⊐ ⊏⊐ ⊏⊐ ⊏⊐ ⊏⊐ ⊏⊐ ⊏⊐ ⊏⊐ ⊏⊐ ⊏⊐ ⊏⊐ ⊏⊐	⊿	⚰ ⚰ ⚰ ⚰ ⚰ ⚰ ⚰
1937	⊏⊐ ⊏⊐ ⊏⊐ ⊏⊐ ⊏⊐ ⊏⊐ ⊏⊐ ⊏⊐ ⊏⊐ ⊏⊐ ⊏⊐ ⊏⊐ ⊏⊐ ⊏⊐ ⊏⊐ ⊏⊐ ⊏⊐	⟋	⚰ ⚰ ⚰ ⚰ ⚰ ⚰

number of deaths in motoring accidents has scarcely reached those of the thirties. In a frantic effort to reduce this slaughter, the government introduced signs of all kinds—cross roads, bends, steep hills and many others—speed limits, and traffic lights at busy cross roads. The Minister of Transport, Mr. Hore-Belisha, devised an orange ball on a black-and-white pole to indicate where pedestrians should cross the road—the forerunner of the present zebra crossings (which have retained the Belisha beacon).

The increase of motor cars allowed people to move further away from their work, and middle class people especially tended to build new houses on the roads leading from the towns in which their offices or shops were situated. There were few rules about building, and provided a man had enough money, he could build more or less what he fancied. So, a long stream of houses of all shapes and sizes straggled along both sides of the main roads, further and further into the country, until they often joined up with the stream coming from the next town. This was called ribbon development.

More houses; more amusements; more holidays; more radio; cheaper goods, food and clothing: for all those except the unemployed and those in poorer jobs, the late thirties seemed a very comfortable period indeed. But those who could read the signs realised that the dream would soon be shattered, and at a single blow most of these luxuries would vanish for more than ten years after the beginning of World War 2.

1. Why was there a severe trade depression in the early 1930s?
2. Which parts of Britain were most affected by this slump in trade? Why did these parts suffer most?
3. What was the 'dole'? How much was it per week?
4. What effect did paying 'dole' have on the government?
5. What measures did the government take to counteract this?
6. What good effects and what bad effects did the events in Germany, Italy and Spain in the mid-1930s have?
7. Why did the standard of living rise in the second half of the 1930s? What forms did this improvement take?
8. What were the main amusements of the 1930s?
9. Give three reasons for the sharp rise in the number of deaths on the roads in the mid-1930s.
10. What measures did the government take to prevent this rise?
11. What advantages and disadvantages did the increase in the number of cars have?
12. What is ribbon development? Was this desirable or not?

Encyclopaedia work
13. Which political parties were in power during the depression?
14. Find out what the average weekly wages are for the current year for the trades listed on page 64.
15. How much unemployment benefit would be paid to day to (a) a single man, (b) a married man with three children?
16. How many unemployed are there today? What fraction of the working population is this?
17. Find out if there are any areas of ribbon development in your district.
18. Draw the latest fashions of 1931 and 1939 and compare them with those of the mid-1920s and of today.

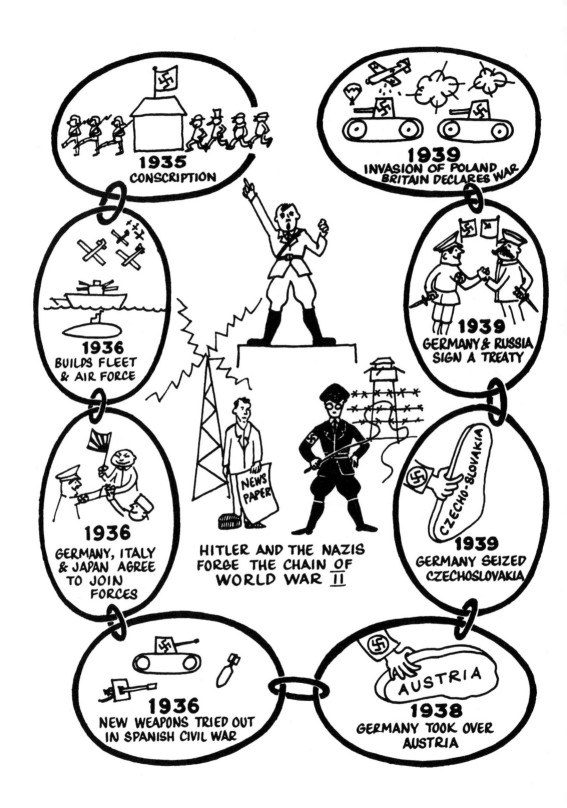

1935 CONSCRIPTION

1939 INVASION OF POLAND BRITAIN DECLARES WAR

1936 BUILDS FLEET & AIR FORCE

1939 GERMANY & RUSSIA SIGN A TREATY

1936 GERMANY, ITALY & JAPAN AGREE TO JOIN FORCES

NEWS PAPER

HITLER AND THE NAZIS FORGE THE CHAIN OF WORLD WAR II

CZECHO-SLOVAKIA

1939 GERMANY SEIZED CZECHOSLOVAKIA

1936 NEW WEAPONS TRIED OUT IN SPANISH CIVIL WAR

AUSTRIA

1938 GERMANY TOOK OVER AUSTRIA

10

THE ROAD TO WORLD WAR 2

Once the Nazis had complete control of Germany at home, they turned their thoughts to seizing territory abroad. But first they had to build up their armed forces, especially those forbidden by the Treaty of Versailles. The dreaded Gestapo, under its chief, Himmler, prevented any voices inside the country being raised: the press and radio, under the leadership of Josef Goebbels, poured a never-ending stream of lying propaganda to the whole world about the good intentions of the Nazi party, how the German people had been wickedly treated by the peacemakers at Versailles, and the wickedness of the Jews.

In 1935 Hitler announced that Germany was no longer bound by the treaty, and ordered all Germans to serve for two years in the army (18–20). Before this they had to work for six months in a labour camp, and after their military service they were placed on the reserve for fourteen years, with frequent training sessions and camps.

Hitler saw in Italy's fascist dictator, Mussolini, a man after his own heart. In 1935 Italy, wishing to build up an empire of her own which would rival in importance the empires of Britain, France and Germany, had attacked Abyssinia (Ethiopia). The spears and bows and arrows of the Abyssinians were no match for the guns, poison gas and bombers of the Italians. Within a few months, Abyssinia was added to Italy's empire. Her unprovoked attack on an almost defenceless state shocked the whole world except Hitler. The two countries, Germany and Italy, agreed to cooperate in the future and set up what they called the Rome–Berlin Axis. (During the war Germany and her partners were often called the Axis Powers.)

In 1936 Hitler began to build a large fleet, mainly of submarines and small, but extremely powerful warships, and a huge air force. Both of these had been forbidden by the Treaty of Versailles. In the same year he signed a treaty with Italy and Japan under which all promised to help each other to fight against communism.

Both of these moves had been of the Nazis' making, but in 1936 came a stroke of luck, of which they took full advantage. A bitter civil war broke out in Spain between the government, which was corrupt, and part of the army, which was no better, under General Franco. Soon the whole of Spain was blazing with savage atrocities, and the world for the first time

How Germany built up her forces between 1933 and 1939. The strength of the British forces is given for comparison.

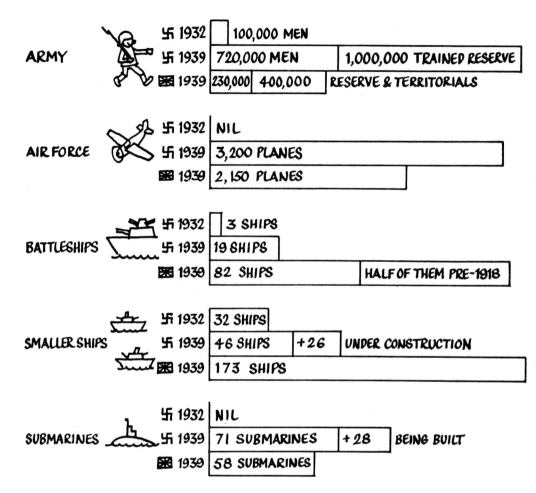

ARMY
- 卐 1932 | 100,000 MEN
- 卐 1939 | 720,000 MEN | 1,000,000 TRAINED RESERVE
- 🏴 1939 | 230,000 | 400,000 | RESERVE & TERRITORIALS

AIR FORCE
- 卐 1932 | NIL
- 卐 1939 | 3,200 PLANES
- 🏴 1939 | 2,150 PLANES

BATTLESHIPS
- 卐 1932 | 3 SHIPS
- 卐 1939 | 19 SHIPS
- 🏴 1939 | 82 SHIPS | HALF OF THEM PRE-1918

SMALLER SHIPS
- 卐 1932 | 32 SHIPS
- 卐 1939 | 46 SHIPS | +26 | UNDER CONSTRUCTION
- 🏴 1939 | 173 SHIPS

SUBMARINES
- 卐 1932 | NIL
- 卐 1939 | 71 SUBMARINES | +28 | BEING BUILT
- 🏴 1939 | 58 SUBMARINES

learned what warfare with large-scale air bombing was like. Germany and Italy helped the rebels with men, money and, most important, with weapons, partly because the Spanish government was friendly with communist Russia, partly because Franco held similar political views to those of Hitler and Mussolini and wanted to set up a fascist dictatorship, but mainly because it was a wonderful opportunity to try out the new tanks, aeroplanes and other weapons under real battle conditions. When World War 2 did break out this experience proved very valuable to Germany, for whereas British equipment often broke down and developed faults, the Nazis had well-tried and well-tested weapons, and had worked out new ways of fighting.

1937 was a year of relative peace abroad as far as Germany was concerned, except for helping in the Spanish war, but production of armaments and training was speeded up ready for the next step to the coming struggle.

Hitler had long had his eyes on the neighbouring state of Austria, whose people speak German and who are, in many ways, very like the Germans. An Austrian Nazi party had been organised, and had attempted to seize power in 1934 by murdering the Chancellor, Dr. Dollfuss, but had failed.

This extract from the *Annual Register* of 1934 shows the Nazi methods of getting rid of people, even in foreign countries, who opposed them. Dr. Dollfuss was the Chancellor of Austria, and opposed the Nazis in his own country.

> "At 10 a.m. the Nazis selected to execute the plot assembled in a German gymnastic hall, put on the uniforms of the Heimwehr (Home Guard) and regular soldiers (i.e. of the Austrian army), drew arms and mounted motor lorries.
>
> Shortly before 1 p.m. the motor lorries with the rebels drove up to the Chancellery and were allowed past the sentries. Only when they were inside did the rebels reveal their true mission. But they failed in their true objective, which was to arrest the Cabinet as a whole (most of them had gone to lunch, the *Annual Register* explains)... Inside the Chancellery Dr. Dollfuss was shot by one of the Nazis . . . as he was trying to escape. His wounds were roughly bandaged, but the rebels refused to allow anyone to leave the building to summon a doctor and the Chancellor died while in their hands..."

By 1938, however, the Austrian Nazis had become very powerful, so that when Hitler demanded that the country should be handed over to Germany—and backed up his demand by moving a quarter of a million soldiers and 700 planes to the frontier, the country was handed over without a shot being fired. The Fifth Column (Austrian Nazis) had seized key points such as telephone exchanges, railway junctions and police headquarters so that any resistance was almost impossible. The other countries of the world were horrified at this unprovoked seizure, but did nothing about it as Hitler promised that once German-speaking Austria was in the German empire he would never attack another country.

Within a few months, however, he demanded that large parts of Czechoslovakia should be handed to Germany as many of the people who lived there were Germans. This was true—but the Germans were the descendants of people who had migrated there years before, some as long ago as the Middle Ages.

Perhaps Hitler was more interested in the great Skoda armaments factory in Czechoslovakia, which could soon be his, than in the three million German-speaking people, but whatever the reason, the Nazi army and airforce began massing for the usual invasion. This time Europe was alarmed, and the British Prime Minister, Mr. Neville Chamberlain, flew to meet Hitler. After a series of conferences between the Germans, British and French at Munich, Hitler promised—again—that once he had those areas of Czechoslovakia he wanted, he would not fight nor ask for any more territory. Without asking Czechoslovakia herself, Britain and France gave the German-speaking districts to Hitler, and betrayed by the two countries they thought they could trust, the Czechs had to surrender to the mighty armies of Germany.

By 'appeasement'—that is, giving a bully what he wants to keep him quiet—war was avoided at the time. Mr. Chamberlain, who acted in good faith, was hailed as a great man and a giver of peace, but a few, and prominent amongst them Mr. Churchill, called for action to be taken against the tyrant Hitler. Their voices were disregarded—but only for a year, for Hitler's promises were not worth the breath they were uttered with. Six months later, in March 1939, the Nazis demanded the rest of Czechoslovakia, and with massed troops crossed the frontiers. In one day they occupied the capital, Prague.

It soon became obvious that Hitler would strike next at Poland, but Britain and France had now taken a firm stand and had threatened to fight if the Nazis invaded. As Poland was Russia's neighbour, there was a strong possibility that the U.S.S.R. would attack Germany too. Hitler was not ready to meet attacks in the west and in the east at once, so by a surprise treaty of friendship he bought off Russia by offering her large areas of eastern Poland if she remained neutral. Then, with the eastern frontier safe, he attacked.

This is how the *Annual Register* of 1939 describes the invasion:

"At 5.40 a.m. on Friday, September 1st, German troops crossed the frontier into Poland without warning, and with this act of wanton aggression the second great war of the century was started...

By the 20th the war in Poland was over except for the Capital city of Warsaw, which, under its heroic Mayor, Stefan Starzynski, defended itself until September 29th, when, owing to lack of food, water, and ammunition, it was forced to surrender, having endured air bombing and heavy artillery bombardment which laid the city in ruins!"

And this is how the *Annual Register* describes what happened after the capture of Poland:

"Perhaps the most barbarous practice adopted by the Germans was the collective punishment of individual ... crimes. Wherever a German, whether military or civilian, suffered injury, or firearms were

74

alleged to have been possessed by a resident, wholesale executions took place. Thus in Szcuczka, in the district of Lublin, ammunition having been discovered buried in a peasant's field, 200 men were shot and burnt in a shed. At Kopanica the entire population was exterminated ... near Radom, about 1200 persons were massacred in the different villages, a number of which were burnt to the ground . . ."

This time Britain and France did not draw back, but gave Hitler twenty-four hours to withdraw from Poland (the ultimatum to expire on the 3rd of September). Disregarding this warning, and quite confident of victory, he marched forward, and so hurled Europe into World War 2.

---

1. Germany needed an excuse for re-arming. It was also necessary to explain to her people why Germany was in such a poor condition. What did Goebbels use as excuses in his propaganda?
2. How did Hitler manage to build up such a large army of trained men between 1935 and 1939?
3. Why do you think that the German Navy concentrated on the building of submarines rather than heavy battleships? What are the advantages of submarines? (You should consider such things as the element of surprise, cost, striking power, Britain's position as an island, trade routes.)
4. Imagine that you were Hitler at the time of the Civil War in Spain. In what way would you and your Italian allies welcome the chance to take a part? Why would it be advantageous to you? Would it have any effect on a war that might come in the future?
5. What excuses did Hitler make for seizing Austria and Czechoslovakia?
6. What is *appeasement*? What appeasement was offered by Mr. Chamberlain at Munich?
7. Does it pay to 'appease'?
8. What fears did Hitler have about attacking Poland and how did he overcome this problem?

Find out:
(a) What were the Maginot and Siegfried Lines?
(b) What were the International Brigades in the Spanish Civil War? You will find a vivid description of their activities in George Orwell's *Homage to Catalonia* and Ernest Hemingway's *For Whom the Bell Tolls*.
(c) Why is Guernica important? Look it up in an encyclopaedia and say why it is worth mentioning.

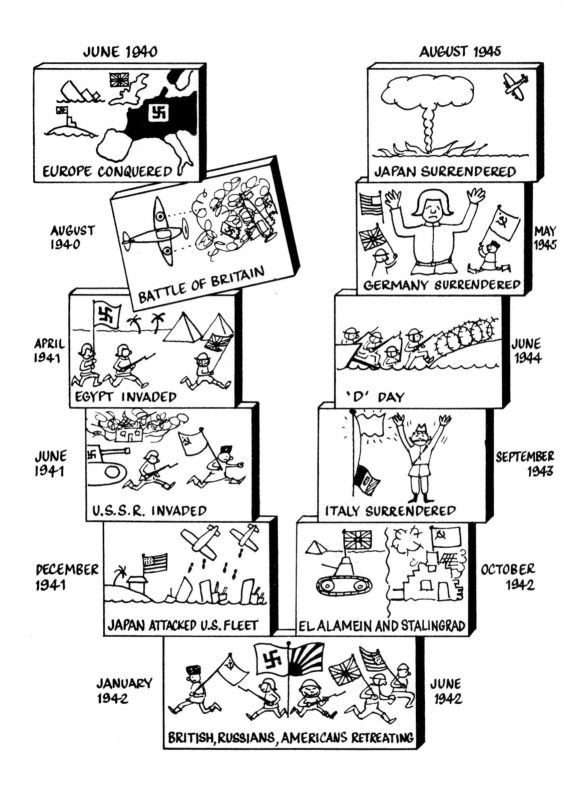

11

WORLD WAR 2

War was declared on Germany in September 1939 when she refused to stop the invasion of Poland, but quite unexpectedly, for six months there was very little fighting except for a few minor air raids and some battles at sea. The British army crossed to France and took up defensive positions along the Franco-Belgian frontier.

Then suddenly, in April 1940, the Nazis struck with their *blitzkrieg*, the 'high-speed war' with fast-moving columns of tanks which they had perfected in the Spanish Civil War, and for which the British and French were unprepared. In two months Denmark, Norway, Holland, Belgium and Northern France had been captured, and only by a miracle did the bulk of the British army manage to escape in a fleet of yachts, launches, paddle-steamers, warships and even rowing boats from Dunkirk.

With almost the whole of northern Europe conquered by the Nazis, Britain was alone, without a single ally except for the Commonwealth countries. Hitler then made plans to complete his conquest by invading England, but first of all, before he could transport his troops across the Channel, he had to destroy the Royal Air Force. With this in view the German Air Force began in the late summer of 1940 a series of massive daylight air raids to destroy the aerodromes in southern England. Throughout August and September the skies above Kent, Surrey, Sussex and Essex were a weaving mass of fighting aeroplanes as the Battle of Britain was fought out between the Spitfires and Hurricanes of the Royal Air Force and the Messerschmitts and Heinkels of the German Luftwaffe. Here, for the first time, Hitler met defeat: his proud air force was completely routed by the outnumbered R.A.F, and the Nazis were compelled to give up their plans for invasion for the time being. Unable to fly in the skies over Britain in the daytime, the Nazis switched to the great night bombing raids—the Blitz—on the cities of England, hoping to force Britain into surrender by the wholesale destruction of cities.

Here is an account of one fight in the Battle of Britain, written by a young pilot, Richard Hillary, who was later killed in the air.

"... in a few seconds we were running for our machines. I climbed into the cockpit of my plane and felt an empty sensation of suspense in the pit of my stomach. For one second time seemed to stand still and I stared blankly in front of me. I knew that that morning I was to kill for the first time. That I might be killed or in any way injured did not occur to me... I knew it could not happen to me. I suppose every pilot knows that, knows that it cannot happen to him: even when he is taking off for the last time, when he will not return, he knows that he cannot be killed. I wondered idly what he was like, this man I would kill. Was he young, was he fat, would he die with the Fuehrer's name on his lips... I would never know. Then I was being strapped in, my mind automatically checking the controls, and we were off.

We ran into them at 18,000 feet, twenty yellow-nosed Messerschmitt 109's, about 500 feet above us. Our squadron strength was eight, and as they came down on us we went into line astern and turned head on to them. Brian Carbury, who was leading the Section, dropped the nose of his machine, and I could almost feel the leading Nazi pilot push forward on the stick to bring his guns to bear. At the same moment Brian hauled hard back on his own control stick and led us over them in a steep climbing turn to the left. In two vital seconds they lost their advantage. I saw Brian let go a burst of fire at the leading plane, saw the pilot put his machine into a half roll, and I knew that he was mine. Automatically I kicked the rudder to the left to get him at right angles, turned the gun-button to 'Fire', and let go in a four-second burst with full deflection. He came right through my sights and I saw the tracer from all eight guns thud home. For a second he seemed to hang motionless; then a jet of red flame shot upwards and he spun out of sight... It had happened... He was dead, and I was alive: it could so easily have been the other way round.

From this flight Broody Benson did not return."

(*The Last Enemy*, by Richard Hillary)

Air raids.
Of every 26 houses in Britain in 1939, by 1945

17 were untouched   8 damaged   1 destroyed

Many Londoners spent every night in the underground stations to escape from the bombing. This is how the *Illustrated London News* described it in 1940:

"... even the unused escalators are providing comfortless perches for the shelterers. People begin to arrive as early as 4 p.m. with their bedding and shopping bags filled with food. By the time the evening rush begins they have already selected their pitches for the night. Business people homeward bound wave from trains to the mothers and children. Some of the older children do their homework using the platforms for a desk for their books. Later on, men, women and children remove their boots and shoes and sleep, despite the thunder of the trains."

In spite of the battering they received the British people held on. The R.A.F. were still masters of our sky.

With the invasion of Britain now postponed, Hitler turned his army to other fields of battle. In April 1941 the Germans, together with their Italian allies, invaded Greece and Yugoslavia, joining the Italians in their occupation of Albania. A month later, despite their treaty of friendship, the Germans attacked Russia. As in the rest of Europe, the Germans seemed unbeatable: the Russians, fighting desperately and losing millions of soldiers and civilians, retreated eastwards, destroying farms, bridges, factories, power stations and even whole cities rather than let them fall into the hands of the enemy. In the south, Greece, Yugoslavia and Albania were quickly overrun. German troops had already, in February 1941, crossed into North Africa to help their Italian allies who were being hard-pressed by the British in the Italian colony of Libya. Here too everything seemed to fall into Hitler's lap: the British were forced back through the desert and Egypt itself was invaded. Although Britain now had an ally in Russia, the outlook was very black indeed.

At the end of 1941, when the situation seemed at its worst, an even heavier blow fell. The Japanese, without warning, attacked the great American naval base of Pearl Harbour in the Hawaiian Islands with bombing planes, and in a few minutes put a whole United States fleet out of action, destroyed scores of aeroplanes on the ground and killed thousands of American servicemen. The United States was now in the war, but she too was forced to retreat by the Japanese. The British colonies of Hong Kong, Malaya, and Burma, the French colony of Indo-China and the Dutch East Indies fell rapidly to the Japanese invaders in some of the most savage and most brutal fighting of the war (see the map of the Far East on page 87).

Early in 1942 the war seemed lost for the British, Russians and Americans. The Germans were almost in Moscow; with their Italian allies they were almost in Cairo, and in the east, India and Australia were almost within the grasp of the Japanese. Then in the space of a few months came three great battles which marked the turning points of all three campaigns, and indeed, of the whole war. In the Pacific the Japanese were beaten by the Americans at the great air-and-sea battle of Midway Island, in Russia the battle for the city of Stalingrad began and in the North African desert at El Alamein the British tanks and artillery soundly defeated the seemingly unbeatable Germans. At Stalingrad for four months the German and Russian armies fought for possession of the city, street by street, house by house, until almost half a million Nazi soldiers were dead or prisoners. The Russians then began to counter-attack, pushing the Germans back towards their own country. In the extreme cold of a Russian winter when the oil froze in the German tanks and some of the Nazi soldiers were still in summer uniforms the troops suffered terribly from the bitter temperature and shortage of all supplies. To help with the coming victory, British and American bombers began night and day air raids on Germany itself. For the first time the German people themselves began to experience the horrors of the total war that they had begun.

By the end of 1943 the whole of North Africa had been cleared of the enemy and the invasion of Italy began. Almost at once the Italian armies surrendered, but the Germans in the country kept up the battle. Mussolini, who fled northwards to his friend Hitler when Italy surrendered, was later captured and shot by some of his own countrymen who hated him. In Russia the great weight of the Red Army forced the Nazis westwards in retreat, and in the Far East the Japanese were slowly being pushed back through the jungles by the British and from the Pacific Islands by the Americans. On every front, except at sea, where the submarines still took a terrible toll of shipping of all kinds, the Nazis and their allies were in retreat. Everyone knew, however, that before Germany could be finally defeated the continent of Europe would have to be invaded. As the Germans had had four years in which to build massive fortifications all along the coast, this was a most formidable task.

In June, 1944, 'D'-Day, the day of the invasion came. British, American and other allied troops went ashore on the coast of Normandy after an immense fleet of ships and aeroplanes had crossed the Channel. Fanning out from the beaches, the allies gradually pushed the German forces back after bitter fighting. One by one the countries of Western Europe were freed, and in the east the Russian armies steadily forged westwards. In May 1945 the British and Americans from the west, and the Russians from the east, met in the centre of Germany itself: Hitler had already committed suicide in his deep air-raid shelter in Berlin, and within a few days the Nazis surrendered.

More troops could now be sent to deal with the Japanese, but as you will read in Chapter 12, before the invasion of Japan itself could take place, the world's first atom bombs had been dropped, and the Japanese, rather than face complete destruction of their islands, surrendered in August, three months after their Nazi friends. World War 2 was over, but the problems it created have not even yet been solved.

When the main countries joined and left the war

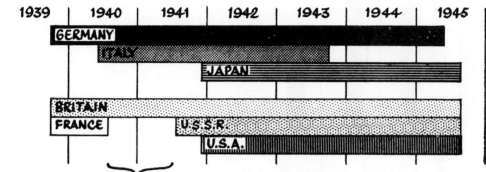

THE CRITICAL YEAR: *BRITAIN ALONE AGAINST GERMANY & ITALY*

Why the war of 1939–45 was called WORLD WAR.

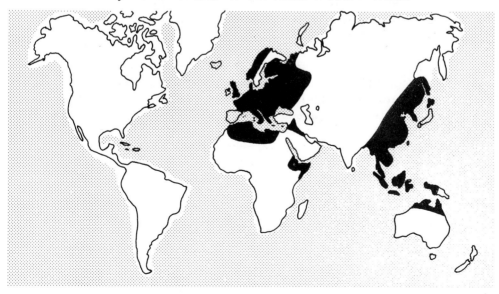

◼ LAND FIGHTING OR AIR RAIDS ▢ FIGHTING AT SEA

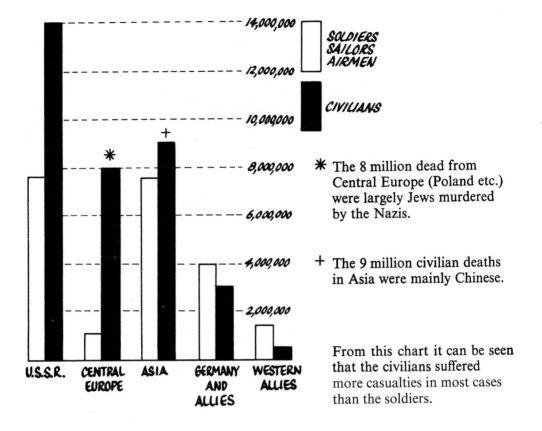

14,000,000

□ SOLDIERS
SAILORS
AIRMEN

12,000,000

■ CIVILIANS

10,000,000

8,000,000   ✱ The 8 million dead from
Central Europe (Poland etc.)
were largely Jews murdered
by the Nazis.

6,000,000

4,000,000   ✛ The 9 million civilian deaths
in Asia were mainly Chinese.

2,000,000

U.S.S.R.   CENTRAL   ASIA   GERMANY   WESTERN
EUROPE   AND   ALLIES
ALLIES

From this chart it can be seen
that the civilians suffered
more casualties in most cases
than the soldiers.

Merchant ships
Of every 19 ships in the British merchant navy in 1939, by 1945 ... only
9 were still afloat...

5 sunk by submarines 2 by aeroplanes ... 2 by warships etc. 1 by mines.

Over half the merchant Navy had been sunk ... and in March 1942 an
average of 9 British ships went to the bottom every day. On the other hand,
about 7 out of every 10 German submarines were sunk.

82

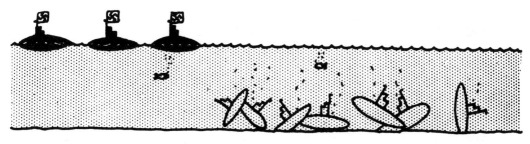

2 NEW HOUSES AND 2 NEW CARS FOR EVERY FAMILY IN BRITAIN

or

100,000 NEW SCHOOLS AND 100,000 NEW HOSPITALS

or

A MOTORWAY *TWICE* ROUND THE WORLD

or

A DECENT STANDARD OF LIVING FOR EVERY-ONE IN THE WORLD

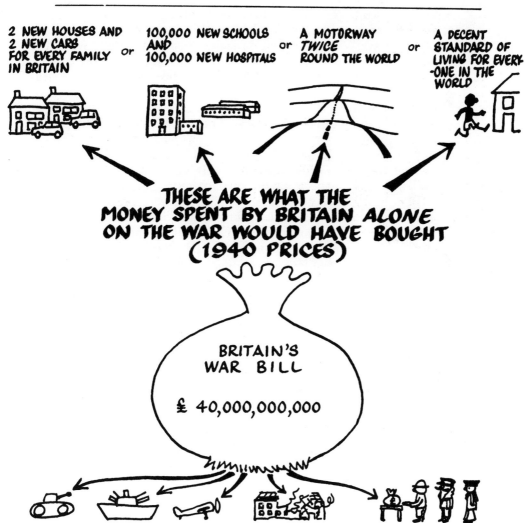

THESE ARE WHAT THE MONEY SPENT BY BRITAIN ALONE ON THE WAR WOULD HAVE BOUGHT (1940 PRICES)

BRITAIN'S WAR BILL

£ 40,000,000,000

INSTEAD IT WAS SPENT ON THESE... AND GERMANY'S BILL WAS MORE THAN *TWICE* THE SIZE OF BRITAIN'S, WHILE AMERICA'S WAS WELL OVER *THREE TIMES* THE SIZE.

THE *MINIMUM* TOTAL COST OF THE WAR HAS BEEN ESTIMATED AT:

£ 390,000,000,000.

1. From your reading of this chapter explain in what ways war is particularly wasteful. You should be able to quote facts and figures. (Look at the diagrams particularly.)
2. In what way was the opening of World War 2 unexpected?
3. What was a 'blitzkrieg' and why was it so successful at first?
4. Imagine that you were a high-ranking member of the Luftwaffe. Write a short speech that you might make to a number of Group Commanders explaining what you aimed to do in the Battle of Britain. Explain why it is necessary to plan an all-out attack on the island.
5. What caused (a) Russia and (b) America to enter the war?
6. Write a short composition explaining why it was so dangerous to invade Europe. What particular difficulties had to be faced? What had tides and currents to do with it? What about security? Why is it always more difficult for the attacker than the defender in such a situation?
7. Would you say it is more important to sink merchant shipping or battleships in time of war? (The chart on page 82—Loss of Shipping—should help you.)
8. In Winston Churchill's book, The Second World War, Vol VI, Chapter One, there is an account of D-Day. It is quite easy and exciting to read and will provide you with some interesting facts. Then write an account of the D-Day landings. Imagine you were a reporter in those stirring times and try to make your account vivid and exciting.
9. Make a time chart showing when each country entered and left the fighting. Mark on it the major battles and other events. (You might find it useful to read *A State of War* in the *Today is History* series published by Hart-Davis Educational, and also pp. 445–7 in Everyman's *Dictionary of Dates*.)
10. What is propaganda? What is its use in wartime?

Find out:
(a) Who were the following: Marshal Pétain; General Montgomery; General Eisenhower; Field Marshal Rommel?
(b) What were the V1 and V2; radar; the fifth column; asdic? What part did each play in the war?
(c) **What was rationing? Find out from adults who lived in wartime what was rationed and why.**

12

JAPAN IN THE 20th CENTURY: THE ATOM BOMB AGE

Until just over a century ago Japan had shut herself off from the rest of the world. The country was ruled with savage cruelty by an emperor and powerful families of military nobles. In most respects Japan was still far back in the middle ages, and allowed few foreigners to enter her islands. Then in 1854 an American fleet forced the Japanese at gunpoint to admit traders from abroad, and once the people of Japan saw the developments and luxuries of the West, there was no stopping them. From about 1867, when the Emperor Mutsuhito came to power, they threw their whole energies into making up for lost time: their industrial spies were everywhere, copying secrets from every country. Factories, railways, roads and telephones appeared as if by magic; western dress was adopted by many and the markets were full of western-type goods at a fraction of the western price. French and German officers were called in to train a new Japanese army, and British experts taught them how to build and sail the huge steel battleships. The population soared, and in the last years of the nineteenth century Japan began to look further than her own boundaries. She seized several small groups of islands in the Pacific Ocean, and meddled in the affairs of the kingdom of Korea, which looked as though it could be a good jumping-off place for any future attack on China or Russia.

In the last years of the nineteenth century (1894–5) Japan felt strong enough to attempt a small-scale war with China, whom she defeated easily. From this victory, Japan gained the island of Formosa, Korea and part of Manchuria. Ten years later she felt powerful enough to pick a quarrel with Russia, and to everyone's surprise sank three Russian fleets sent against her. This was the first glimpse of the power that Japan was to become.

For the next twenty five years Japan quietly built up her power and prosperity by flooding the world markets with cheap goods. Because the Japanese workmen were paid so much less than workers in Europe and America, the factories in Japan could sell their products at prices well below those of other countries. All the while her greedy and ambitious leaders kept their eyes on the rich but sparsely populated lands of China, just across the Sea of Japan. Further away, but even more attractive, were the immensely rich and fertile lands of south east Asia and India. Steadily and quietly, the Japanese built up their army, navy and air force.

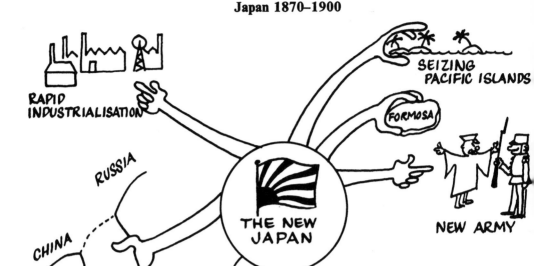

In 1931 Japan struck, and seized the part of northern China called Manchuria: now they had a base on the mainland from which it would be easier to carry out more conquests, and six years later they began a full-scale invasion of the rest of China. From 1937 until 1945 the two countries were continuously at war, with the two Chinese armies (see Chapter 15) gradually retreating further and further into the interior. The Japanese dream of dominating the whole of the Far East, and Australia too, seemed possible.

At the end of 1941, when World War 2 was at its worst for Britain, who, apart from Russia (who was fighting for her own survival), stood alone against Germany and Italy, Japan joined in the battle. Without warning, she sank an American fleet at anchor at Pearl Harbour in the Hawaiian Islands. This brought the United States into the war, but even so there seemed no stopping the Japanese: they swept the Americans out of the Philippine Islands (where they were in command of the armed forces) and the British out of Burma, Malaya and Singapore. They conquered the Dutch East Indies and came within striking distance of India and Australia. The prisoners they captured, both white and coloured, were treated with inhuman cruelty.

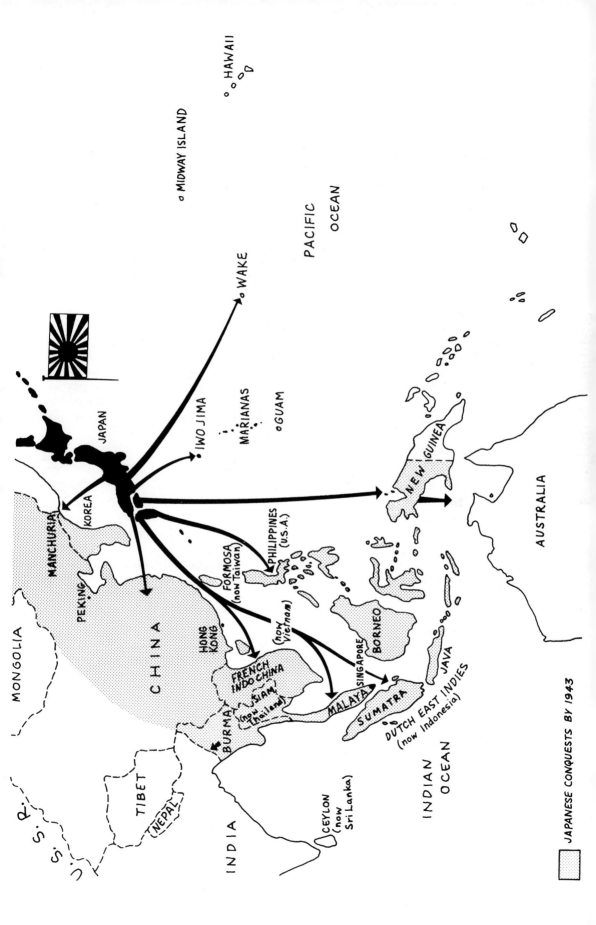

JAPANESE CONQUESTS BY 1943

By 1943, however, the Japanese advance had been halted, and the slow retreat began, with the Emperor's soldiers stubbornly fighting for every inch of jungle and every coral island. When the war ended in Europe in May 1945, more troops could be sent to the Far East, for it was realised that sooner or later the islands of Japan themselves would have to be invaded. The President of the United States (Mr. Truman) now had a terrible decision to make: he could go ahead with an ordinary invasion by sea, as had happened in Europe, and perhaps lose about a million British and American soldiers, or he could use the atomic bomb, which had been developed secretly in America. No one, not even the scientists who had made it, knew exactly what would happen when the bomb was dropped, but they did know its results would be most terrible and destructive, as an experimental test in the deserts of New Mexico in July 1945 had proved.

The President consulted his ally, Attlee (British Prime Minister after Labour's election victory of 1945), then made his decision: on August 6th, 1945, a United States bomber dropped a single bomb on the city of Hiroshima. In a fraction of a second the city was virtually destroyed and 80,000 people were wiped out. Yet still the Japanese army chiefs hesitated, and three days later a second atom bomb was dropped on the city of Nagasaki, with similar results. The Japanese now realised that the whole of their country could easily be destroyed, and they surrendered. World

THE PROBLEM FACING THE AMERICAN PRESIDENT (MR. TRUMAN) IN 1945

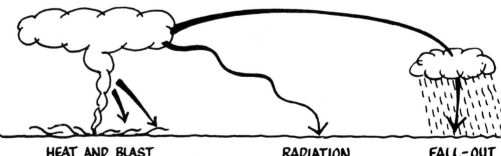

WHY THE ATOMIC BOMB IS SO TERRIBLE IN ITS KILLING POWE

War 2 was over, but the world had entered its most terrible and dangerous age, the Atomic Age.

The moment the bomb explodes a wave of heat, hundreds of thousands of degrees high, burns every living thing out of doors within range, to a cinder. A fraction of a second later an immense blast shatters every building in range. This is all over in a few seconds, but the whole area gives off a deadly radiation which can cause an illness for which there is no known cure. This radiation can last for months, and is given off by stones, buildings—in fact everything within the area of the bomb explosion.

The Atomic Bomb—an argument

Against

1. The most terrible weapon ever. The most powerful form, the hydrogen bomb, can have the force of 80–100 million tons of TNT. Biggest bomb in World War 2 had only 10 tonnes of TNT.
2. Destroys everything within a wide range—good and bad.
3. Radiation and fall-out can kill or deform people and can affect unborn children.
4. There is little protection from its effects. Those who escape the explosion in a deep shelter, can be affected by radiation the moment they come out.
5. In a great atomic world war the whole of the civilised world could be destroyed.
6. Technically, nuclear weapons are not very difficult to make. A small nation or terrorist group which had an atomic bomb could blackmail the rest of the world by threatening to use it.
7. Even peaceful use of atomic power produces waste material which stays very dangerous for hundreds of years. No one yet knows if the methods we use to store this waste will prove to be completely safe in years to come.

For

1. The one argument for atomic weapons may be worth all of those against them. The bomb is so terrible, and any country using it to destroy another country, knows that it would be destroyed also. There is a hope that all countries will be so terrified of an atomic war that they will make sure they never declare war.
2. The immense power contained in an atom bomb can be slowed down and used to make electricity. As coal and oil reserves are used up, atomic power stations may well become the world's chief source of electricity—already scores are in use all over the world. And if there are now submarines powered by atomic energy the day of the atomic passenger liner, the atomic plane and the atomic car is not far off.

When the bomb bursts a cloud of poisonous dust is blown into the atmosphere. This slowly comes to earth in rain storms where it too can cause an incurable illness. The dust can come to earth months or even years later and may even fall in another part of the world. Dust from experimental explosions falls on every part of the earth.

This is a description of Hiroshima after the atomic bomb, taken from the diary of a Japanese doctor at a hospital which was one of the few buildings left standing:

"The streets were deserted except for the dead. Some looked as if they had been frozen to death while in the full action of flight... others lay sprawled as though some giant hand had flung them to their death from a great height.

Hiroshima was no longer a city, but a burnt-out prairie. To the east and to the west everything was flattened... how small Hiroshima was with its houses gone...

... Hundreds of injured people who were trying to escape to the hills passed our house. The sight of them was almost unbearable. Their faces and hands were burnt and swollen; and great sheets of skin had peeled away from their tissues to hang down like rags on a scarecrow. They moved like a line of ants. All through the night, they went past our house, but this morning they had stopped. I found them lying so thick on both sides of the road that it was impossible to pass without stepping on them...'

'... The sight of the soldiers, though, was more dreadful than the dead people floating down the river. I came on to I don't know how many, burned from the hips up; and where the skin had peeled, their flesh was wet and mushy... And they had no faces! Their eyes, noses and mouths had been burned away, and it looked like their ears had melted off. It was hard to tell front from back... The way they were burned, I wonder if they didn't have their coats off when the bomb exploded...'

'... Between the Red Cross Hospital and the centre of the city I saw nothing that wasn't burned to a crisp. Tramcars were standing at Kawaya-cho and Kamiya-cho and inside were dozens of bodies, blackened beyond recognition. I saw fire reservoirs filled to the brim with dead people ... in one reservoir there were so many dead people there wasn't room for them to fall over. They must have died sitting in the water..."

The doctor, who was badly wounded himself, describes vividly conditions immediately after the explosion and for the next six weeks as the radiation sickness began to kill off the survivors. If you do not understand why the American president hesitated before making the decision to use the bomb, read the whole book, which may be in your local library. It is

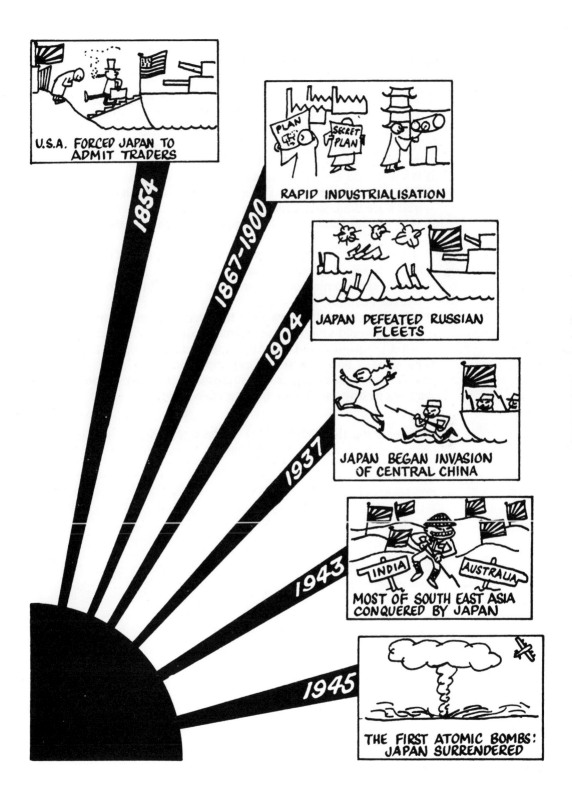

U.S.A. FORCED JAPAN TO ADMIT TRADERS

1854

RAPID INDUSTRIALISATION

1867-1900

JAPAN DEFEATED RUSSIAN FLEETS

1904

JAPAN BEGAN INVASION OF CENTRAL CHINA

1937

MOST OF SOUTH EAST ASIA CONQUERED BY JAPAN

1943

THE FIRST ATOMIC BOMBS: JAPAN SURRENDERED

1945

called *Hiroshima Diary*, by Michihiko Hachiya, published by Victor Gollancz.

---

1. The aim of this exercise is to write a composition entitled *Japan*. Write notes answering the following questions and then join all your answers together to write the completed four-paragraph composition.
  (a) Why had Japan not developed as much as many other countries by the middle of the nineteenth century?
  (b) What started the rise of Japan as a modern industrial state?
  (c) Why did Japan find it easier and quicker to become a fully industrial state than, say, Britain or France?
  (d) Why was Japan able to sell her goods more cheaply than most countries?
2. Read through pages 551–559 of Winston Churchill's THE SECOND WORLD WAR, Volume VI, and then answer the following questions:
  (a) Why is the atomic bomb so much more terrible than ordinary explosive weapons?
  (b) Why were the Allies unwilling to use the atomic bomb when they knew it would save the lives of many allied service men?
  (c) What precautions did the Allies take before dropping the bomb?
  (d) How many bombs were to be dropped on Japan?
3. What is there is this chapter that suggests that nuclear weapons may be a blessing in disguise despite their terrible power?

Find out:
(a) What part did these places play in the war: Corregidor; Singapore; Okinawa; the Burma Road; the Burma-Siam Railway?
(b) Who were: the Chindits; kamikaze pilots?

13

THE UNITED NATIONS

Towards the end of World War 2, Britain, Russia and the United States realised that something must be done to prevent such a catastrophe ever happening again. After a number of meetings of President Franklin D. Roosevelt of America, Joseph Stalin of Russia and Winston Churchill it was decided to form a great club of the nations, rather on the lines of the League of Nations, but, it was hoped, without the weaknesses of the old League. Here, quarrels and other problems between countries could be settled without fighting, for, although Mr. Roosevelt was at that time the only one of the three who knew of the existence of the atom bomb, all agreed that science had made war too terrible to contemplate again. So the United Nations Organisation was born, and a huge skyscraper was built in New York for its headquarters.

Representatives of all member countries (most of the countries in the world belong—142 in all) meet once a year at the General Assembly to discuss general matters such as electing the Secretary General, choosing the members of the many committees and considering applications by new countries for membership. Perhaps the most important job is selecting the Secretary General, for he is the key man in the whole organisation. Up to date there have been four Secretaries—Trygve Lie of Norway (1946–53), Dag Hammarskjöld of Sweden (1953–61) who was killed in an aeroplane crash while on U.N. business in the Congo, U Thant of Burma (1961-1971), and Dr. Kurt Waldheim of Austria who took up office in 1972.

The most important of the U.N's committees is the Security Council, whose main task is to try to keep peace in the world. It consists of five permanent members—Britain, France, the United States, Russia and China (see Chapter 15)—and ten other members chosen to give a representative geographical distribution of nations. Each of these countries serves on the Security Council for two years, half retiring each year.

If two nations look like starting a war, or have already done so, the Security Council tries to persuade them to stop. If this fails, the council can ask all other member countries to stop trading with the quarrelling states until shortage of supplies forces them to give up the war. As a last resort, the council can send an army made up of soldiers from several member countries to the troubled area to stop the fighting if possible, or at least, to prevent it from spreading into a world war. United Nations armies have fought in Korea, Cyprus and the Congo, and in these three alone have prevented what could easily have developed into World War 3.

Another important committee is the International Court of Justice which meets in Holland. Fifteen judges, each one from a different nation, sit to settle points of law which arise between countries and which could lead to war. The Court decides such issues as where the exact frontiers between countries run and how near to one country's coast foreign fishing boats may catch fish.

As well as its main job of keeping peace, the U.N. tries to help countries with primitive economies and those not as developed or rich as Britain, Russia or America to improve their standards of living. It has also set up a number of organisations to help countries to be more friendly with one another and to get them to work and trade together. Here are some of the more important departments.

Food and Agriculture Organisation (FAO). This advises these countries on which crops to grow and how to manage them. It experiments to find better varieties of plants and how to breed better animals. It studies pests such as locusts and crop diseases and tries to find ways of controlling them.

World Health Organisation (WHO). The doctors and scientists of WHO teach less developed countries how to run hospitals and fight disease. They show mothers in backward parts of the world how to look after their children, they run clinics and give inoculations against diseases, especially in tropical countries.

International Bank. This lends money to countries which are short of money for important developments and improvements such as huge dams or building.

Educational, Scientific and Cultural Organisation (UNESCO). This tries to get countries to share each others' books, films, music, sport and scientific discoveries so that the people will understand each other better and be less likely to fight. It also helps to educate the illiterate people in underdeveloped countries.

Children's Fund (UNICEF). This specialises in helping underfed, ill-treated or neglected children all over the world.

International Civil Aviation Organisation (ICAO) sees that all the air liners of its member countries are kept in first class condition and have all possible safety devices. It also organises search and rescue operations.

94

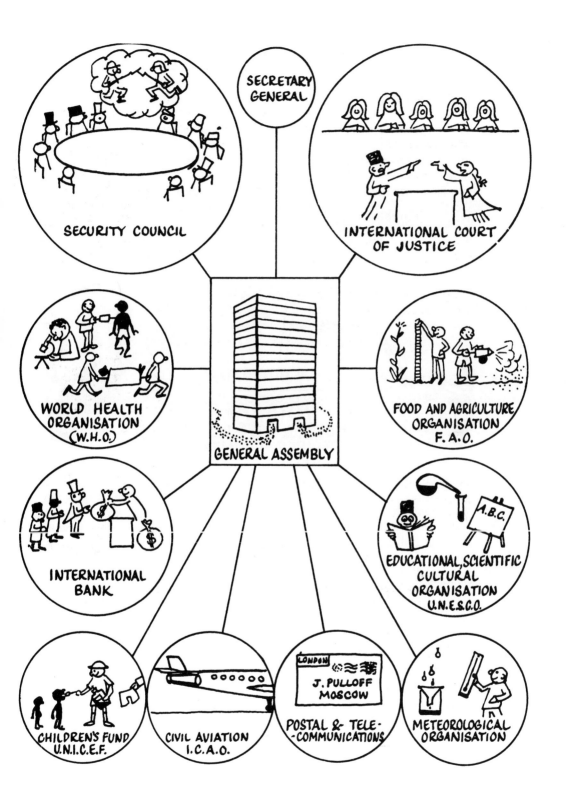

Universal Postal Union and International Telecommunications Union.
Members agree to carry each others' letters, telegrams and telephone
messages although all the money for the stamps or phone calls goes to the
country where the letter was posted, or from which the call was made.

World Meteorological Organisation (WMO). Scientists and meteorologists
of all the countries belonging to WMO send records of winds, temperature
and other information to each other so that better weather forecasts can
be made.

There are now (1976) 142 members of the United Nations:

(a) 40–50 countries who usually vote with U.S.A.
(b) 12–15 countries who usually vote with Russia.
(c) The remainder, mainly in Africa and Asia, vote sometimes with one
side, sometimes with the other.

The way these undecided or "uncommitted" countries vote is of great
importance as any resolution to be passed in the General Assembly must
get $\frac{2}{3}$ of all the votes cast. If the vote is about something which one side
wants and the other does not, there are sometimes angry scenes as the
United States and Russia try to get the African and Asian members to vote
for their point of view.

China and the United Nations
When the United Nations was formed in 1945, General Chiang Kai-shek
and his Nationalist army were in control of much of China, and he signed
on behalf of his country. In the civil war which followed between Chiang
and the communist army of Mao Tse-tung and Chou En-lai, the Nationalists
were beaten, and in 1949 Chiang with the remains of his army took refuge in
the island of Formosa (or Taiwan) 160 km off the coast. His representative
still took the seat for the whole of China at the United Nations while the
People's Republic on the mainland, with over 500 million people, or almost
a quarter of the world's population, was not allowed to attend largely
because the U.S.A. objected.

THE LEAGUE OF NATIONS   UNITED NATIONS

MANY IMPORTANT COUNTRIES, INCLUDING U.S.A., DID NOT JOIN

EVERY IMPORTANT NATION IS A MEMBER

A NUMBER OF NATIONS WALKED OUT WHEN THEY DID NOT AGREE

THEIR IS NO PROVISION FOR A MEMBER TO LEAVE THE U.N. THOUGH MEMBERS MAY BE EXPELLED

THE LEAGUE HAD NO ARMED FORCE TO STOP WAR

MEMBERS PROVIDE SOLDIERS FOR SPECIAL TASKS

For years the bitter quarrel dragged on over who should represent China, who was a permanent member of the Security Council. The obvious answer that both Taiwan and mainland China should have members was ruled out because Mao refused to send a delegation if Chiang's men were still there, and the U.S.A. vetoed any resolution which took away Taiwan's seat to give to the communists.

When the People's Republic became involved in border skirmishes with India in 1963 and the following year exploded a nuclear bomb the world realised just how dangerous it was to have such a powerful nation outside the United Nations where no pressure could be brought to bear on her. At last, in 1971, the U.S.A. realised that mainland China could no longer be kept out and in a sudden change of heart dropped her earlier attitude when the application for membership by the People's Republic came up. By a large majority in November 1971 the delegates of Communist China were accepted as the true representatives of the Chinese people, and those of Taiwan were expelled. By a strange irony at almost the first meeting they attended the members of the People's Republic found themselves voting with the U.S.A. against Russia in the debates on the Bangladesh War in India.

1. Why did the countries of the world decide that the UNITED NATIONS was such a necessary organisation?

2. Why is the Security Council the most important committee of the UN?

3. What is an *uncommitted* country? Name one or two and show how they are uncommitted.

4. What lessons did the founders of the United Nations learn from the weaknesses of the League of Nations?

Find out:

(a) Which countries are not members of the United Nations? (Three are in Europe.)

(b) Draw the Flag of the UN. What does it represent?

(c) What are the following? Say what work each does:
    (a) UNESCO; (b) WHO; (c) FAO; (d) UNICEF.

(d) Make a list of the UN agencies (you can get details from The United Nations, London Information Centre, 14 Stratford Place, London, W.1). From the list choose a number of the agencies and find out what work they do. Collect posters, pictures, photographs. Write notes and compositions on what you discover. Aim eventually at an exhibition entitled: THE UNITED NATIONS, its work and influence.

(e) The United Nations has successfully intervened in the squabbles of various countries. Sometimes it has been unsuccessful. Find out what you can about the work of the UN in the Congo and try to decide whether the UN succeeded in its work.

14

AMERICA, RUSSIA, AND THE COLD WAR

When World War 2 ended, the United States and the Soviet Union were the most powerful nations on earth with the United States probably the wealthiest. Although both China and India had far more people than America or Russia, the United States and the Soviet Union were much more highly developed and industrialised. The Americans, too, already had atomic weapons, and the Russians, largely because of brilliant spies, soon developed theirs.

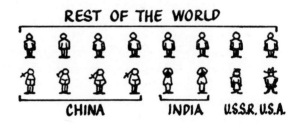

OF EVERY 16 PEOPLE IN THE WORLD: 4 ARE CHINESE
2 ARE INDIAN
1 IS AMERICAN
1 IS RUSSIAN

Areas of the larger countries

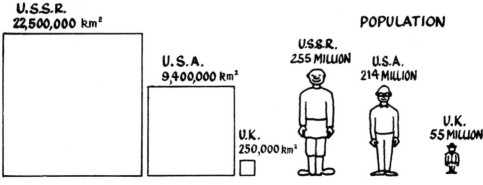

U.S.S.R.
22,500,000 km²

U.S.A.
9,400,000 km²

U.K.
250,000 km²

POPULATION

U.S.S.R.
255 MILLION

U.S.A.
214 MILLION

U.K.
55 MILLION

The two great powers glared at each other across the world, for although they had united to fight against the Nazis, in almost everything else they are completely different.

First of all, the United States believes that a country should be run on a Capitalist system—that is, all industry, business and agriculture should be owned by private people and firms. They believe that competition between rival factories or shops or farms will cause prices to fall and make the firms more efficient. If factory A is selling cars at £500, then factory B must sell theirs at the same price, or an even lower one, if they wish to remain in business. In order to make their cars for £500, factory B may have to scrap its old-fashioned machinery and install modern, more efficient equipment.

The Russians, on the other hand, believe in Socialism—that is, that everything should belong to the state and should be run by the government on behalf of the people. The Americans believe that any man who wishes to do so should be allowed to start a business and employ people to work for him. If he is hard-working enough, or skilful enough he may make a profit. If he pays his workmen £20 a week and makes £1000 a week profit for himself, he should, the Americans say, be allowed this as a reward for his intelligence and for the risk he is taking with his money.

The Russians believe that this system is wrong, and that no private person should be allowed to make a profit from the work of other citizens. If the labours of the ordinary people are to make a profit, then it should, they say, belong to the government, who will use it for the good of everyone in the country by building and running hospitals and schools, by paying for defence, communications and all the other needs of a country. So, all Russian factories and businesses (except for a few small one-man concerns) belong to the state, and their profits, instead of going into the pockets of one owner, or even a body of shareholders, go to the state.

America believes in the law of supply and demand. If, for example, too many firms are making washing machines, shops will have to keep reducing prices to try to sell them until they reach a level at which they are making a loss. As there is not enough profit in washing machines, factories will stop making them. If, on the other hand, there are only a few coloured television sets on the market, many people will want them. Firms will be able to push their prices higher and higher, as someone will be prepared to pay. The high prices for the sets will attract other firms to make them and as soon as more appear in the shops, the prices will start to fall.

Russia believes in a controlled economy. The government tries to work out how many cars or perambulators will be needed for that year, and sets the factory to make that number, which are sold at a controlled price. This, they say, avoids wasteful over-production, and under-production with its high prices.

If, in America, one trade or profession, or even one district, finds itself short of workers, then more must be attracted by higher wages or better

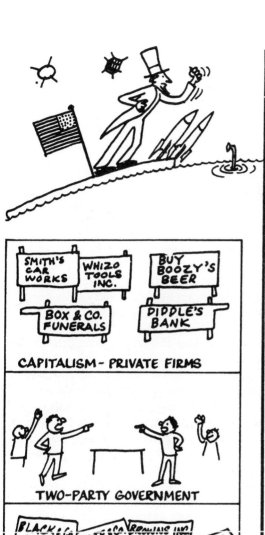

CAPITALISM – PRIVATE FIRMS

SMITH'S CAR WORKS · WHIZO TOOLS INC. · BUY BOOZY'S BEER · BOX & CO. FUNERALS · DIDDLE'S BANK

TWO-PARTY GOVERNMENT

FREE ECONOMY

BLACK & Co · WHITE & Co · BROWNS INC · 20¢ OFF · 50¢ OFF · FREE OFFER · GREEN · ½ PRICE

GREAT DIFFERENCES IN WEALTH BUT MAJORITY WELL OFF

SOCIALISM – STATE OWNERSHIP

STATE CAR FACTORY No. 2. · GOVERNMENT TOOL WORKS No. 6. · THE PEOPLE'S BREWERY · GOVERNMENT GROCERY SHOP · STATE BANK No. 20.

ONE-PARTY GOVERNMENT

CONTROLS

FIXED PRICE 50 R. · CONTROLLED PRICE 5 R. · CONTROLLED PRICE 25 R.

WEALTH MORE EQUALLY SHARED BUT GENERALLY LESS THAN U.S.A.

OVER-PRODUCTION   UNDER-PRODUCTION   CONTROLLED PRODUCTION

conditions. In a similar situation in Russia workers might be ordered by the government to go to that particular job or area. The American, too, can earn as much as his trade union can force out of his employer: if necessary, he can go on strike until the wages are increased or his hours shortened. In Russia, the wages and hours are fixed by law and strikes are, in practice, impossible.

As a result of all this there are much greater differences in wealth in the United States than in the Soviet Union. In America there are powerful business men whose incomes are several million dollars a year (one estimate is that one person in every 600 is a millionaire), but there are also some desperately poor people almost on the starvation level. From their relatively high wages the Americans have to provide for many services such as hospitals and medical care, which the Russians are given by the state. In the Soviet Union there are no millionaires, but there are very few, by their standards, who are desperately poor. However, the standard of living in America is, on the average, much higher than in Russia. There is, for example, one motor vehicle for every two people in the U.S.A.: in the U.S.S.R. there are probably 50 people to every car.

In the matter of government, the two countries are completely different. America has two main political parties, the Republicans and the Democrats. Each has its own ideas on the way the country should be governed, and it is up to the people to decide at election time which one they want. The Russians have only one party, the Communists. They say that this is quite fair as the Communists know what is best for the vast majority of people. Any other party would be in the interest of only a minority of the population and must, therefore, not be allowed.

The governments of the U.S.A. and the U.S.S.R.
In America *most* people over 18 are allowed to vote in elections for President, the Senate and the House of Representatives, but not all. The actual details of those entitled to elect their representatives varies from state to state: some demand that the person must have lived in that state for a

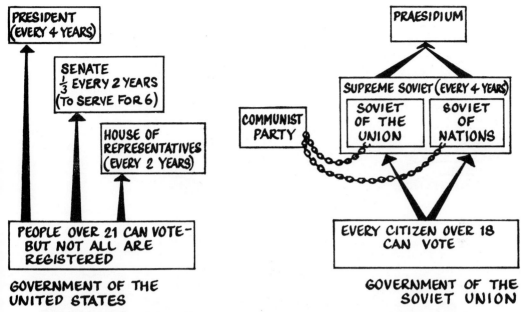

GOVERNMENT OF THE UNITED STATES

GOVERNMENT OF THE SOVIET UNION

certain number of months—or even years—before he is allowed to vote. Twenty of the states demand that voters must be able to read a certain passage from the United States constitution; still others insist that only those who pay certain taxes can vote, and one, Alabama, compels all voters to take an anti-Communist oath. The states which have the strictest regulations about who can and who cannot vote are usually in the south of the United States, and many of these laws are devised to prevent the negroes from taking part in the elections.

Every two years the people elect a House of Representatives, which is similar in function to our own House of Commons, and every two years they choose one-third of the Senate, which is vaguely like our House of Lords except that its members are elected. Every four years the people elect, by a rather roundabout method, a President. As the House of Representatives and the Senate are chosen at different times it is possible for one to have a majority of Republicans, and the other a majority of Democrats. This can make the passing of laws difficult.

In Russia every citizen over eighteen (except certain criminals and lunatics) is allowed to vote for the Supreme Soviet, which is elected every four years. The Supreme Soviet consists of two councils (soviets)—the Soviet of the Union, which is elected on the basis of one member for every 300,000 of the population, and the Soviet of the Nations, which consists of members sent by each individual republic of the U.S.S.R., in proportion to its size.

The Supreme Soviet is too large (about 800 in the Soviet of the Union and 600 in the Soviet of the Nations) to work satisfactorily as one body

103

so it chooses a small committee, called the Praesidium, to run the most important business. The Supreme Soviet meets only to agree to, or reject, the decisions made by the Praesidium.

Every member of all of these councils must be a communist, and must be nominated by the Communist Party, so that is really the Party which controls the running of the country. The head of the Communist Party (the Secretary) is therefore the most powerful man in Russia.

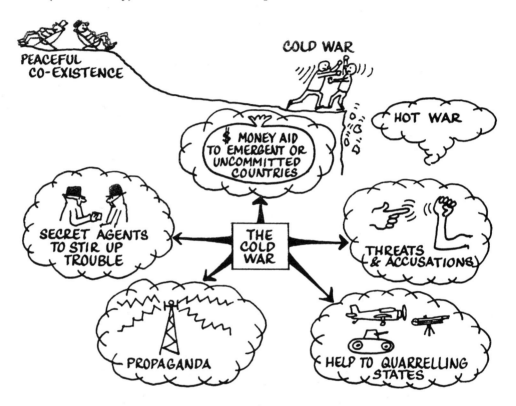

The cold war and peaceful co-existence

When two nations are so powerful and so different as America and Russia are, they are bound to be suspicious and afraid of each other. Both wish to increase their influence and trade, and both hope that more and more countries will turn to their way of life. In the past these differences would have been settled by fighting, but today everyone realises that 'Hot war' with nuclear weapons would destroy both sides. So the U.S.A. and the U.S.S.R. have resorted to 'Cold war', which is really a war of nerves. By bluffing or threatening actual war, by helping small quarrelling states, by sending out streams of propaganda in all languages, by stirring up trouble in unsettled countries and by giving large sums of money to underdeveloped countries they can often get what they want without turning to bloodshed. Threats and accusations, if shouted loudly enough, will often make the opposing side give up its plans, but there is a very great danger that if the threatened side calls the other's bluff and continues what it was doing, the accuser has to carry out his threats or else look a fool in the eyes of the world. All the time the 'cold war' is being carried on on the very edge of 'hot war'—one small slip or miscalculation and the whole world would be plunged into the unimaginable horrors of a nuclear conflict. In fact, on several occasions when full-scale fighting between the two giants seemed almost certain, Britain or other states which have little power in a military sense, but which have considerable influence in the world, have managed to suggest a peaceful solution.

The alternative to the 'cold war' is peaceful co-existence. Two such different ways of life as communism and what the western countries call 'democracy' can never be close friends, but the two can say to each other, "We do not agree with your ways, and we believe them to be wrong, but if you will leave us alone to do what we think best, we will not interfere with you". This, it seems, is the only solution to the present situation with a world divided so sharply in two.

---

1. Write two paragraphs; in paragraph A explain how a capitalist country runs; and in paragraph B show how a Communist country runs.
2. Explain simply what is meant by the law of supply and demand.
3. From your reading of this chapter, explain why it is so necessary for the Russians to plan their economy so carefully.
4. What is meant by a two-party system of government? What are the arguments in favour of it?
5. What is a one-party system of government? What are the arguments for it as it is practised in the U.S.S.R.?
6. Although the Russian people vote for members of their parliament, the real power lies in the hands of the Communist party. Why is this so?
7. The elections for the Senate, the House of Representatives and the President of the United States take place at different times. What problems does this cause?
8. Why do you think that some American states are so strict about the people they allow to vote in elections? What restrictions do they make?
9. Why is the Supreme Soviet in some ways an unsatisfactory body for making laws? And how do the Russians overcome this?
10. What are the alternatives to the cold war?

Find out:
(a) How many members are there in: (i) The House of Commons; (ii) the House of Representatives; (iii) the Senate?
(b) What are (i) the DEW line, (ii) the 'hot' line, (iii) Polaris submarines, (iv) the ICBM?

(c) In an encyclopaedia look up each of the following and make notes on them: Kruschev, Stalin, Karl Marx, Lenin, Kosygin.

(d) What is meant by the phrase 'The Iron Curtain'? What countries lie behind it?

15

CHINA'S PATH SINCE 1900

When the twentieth century began China was very backward indeed by western standards. Although in the past she had been one of the greatest nations on earth, there had been little progress for centuries, and most of her five or six hundred million people lived lives little better than those of animals. This vast country was supposed to be ruled by the emperor and his nobles, but in the distant provinces local lords and chiefs were the real masters.

At the end of the nineteenth century, too, many westerners—British, French, Germans, Belgians, Austrians, Italians and Russians—had been allowed to enter China to build railways and set up factories and to develop trade. Each country had been given by the emperor an area in which to work, but the westerners treated this almost as a colony. The bitter hatred of the Chinese towards the 'foreign devils' who were exploiting the country was even greater than their hatred of the unjust, cruel Chinese rulers. The country was ripe for rebellion.

In 1896 a young Chinese doctor, Sun Yat-sen, who believed that the country should be a republic, had led a small scale revolution against the emperor, but had failed. By good luck he managed to escape, and for the next fifteen years he wandered in Japan, America and England trying to get support for his movement. While in London, Dr. Sun, who was to be to China what Lenin was to Russia, was kidnapped by secret agents of the Chinese emperor, but while waiting to be sent back for execution he managed to smuggle a letter out of his prison in the Chinese Embassy to some British friends who helped to get him released.

The kidnapping of Dr. Sun in broad daylight in London sounds like an extract from a far-fetched spy story, but it is perfectly true. Dr. Sun was approached by some Chinese in the street and told that a friend wished to see him. Once inside the building to which he was led, he was imprisoned. This extract from Dr. Sun's own book, tells what happened. He is being interviewed by one of his captors, a Mr. Tang.

"'Your being here,' he (Tang) proceeded, 'means life or death. Do you know that?'

'How?' I asked. 'This is England, not China. What do you propose to do with me? If you wish extradition you must let my imprisonment be known to the British Government, and I do not think the government of this country will give me up.'

107

'We are not going to ask for legal extradition, for you' he replied. 'Everything is ready: the steamer is engaged; you are to be bound and gagged and taken from here so there will be no disturbance... Outside Hong Kong harbour there will be a Chinese gunboat to meet you and you will be transferred to that and taken to Canton for trial and execution.'

During that week (Dr. Sun continues) I had written statements of my plight on any scraps of paper I could get and thrown them out of the window. I had first given them to the servants to throw as my window did not look out on the street; but it was evident that all of them had been retained. I attempted to throw them out at my own window myself and by a lucky shot one fell on the leads of the back premises of the house next door..." (This note unfortunately for Dr. Sun, was found by the Chinese, who then screwed the window up so that he could throw out no more. In the end he managed to persuade a Mr. Cole, who was employed by the Chinese, to take a note. Cole himself was frightened, but his wife wrote to a friend of Sun's, a Mr. Cantlie, as follows.)

"'There is a friend of yours imprisoned in the Chinese Legation here since last Sunday. They intend sending him to China where it is certain they will hang him. It is very sad for the poor man and unless something is done at once he will be taken away and no one will know it. I dare not sign my name, but this is the truth, so believe what I say. Whatever you do must be done at once or it will be too late. His name, I believe, is Lin Yin Sen...'"

Mr. Cantlie at once contacted the British Government and wrote to the newpapers. The following headlines appeared in *The Globe* on October 22nd 1896:

STARTLING STORY. CONSPIRATOR KIDNAPPED IN LONDON. IMPRISONMENT IN CHINESE EMBASSY.

Under this pressure, the Chinese were forced to give up Dr. Sun.

In 1911 the long-awaited revolution broke out in earnest, and Sun Yat Sen hurried back to China to lead the rebels. The emperor and his family were expelled and a republic declared with Dr. Sun as its first president (1918). Unfortunately quarrels soon broke out among the leaders of the new state and Dr. Sun spent much of the next twelve years in exile again, while civil war raged up and down the land. Local war lords seized the territory round their fortresses and set themselves up as independent rulers: brigands terrorised whole provinces—and all the while Sun dreamed of a united China with one government and one capital.

By the time he died in 1925 Dr. Sun had succeeded in restoring peace in a small part of China only. He was followed as leader by Chiang Kai-shek, who like two other powerful men in the party, Chou En-lai and Mao

Tse-tung, had been trained as a communist in Moscow. As soon as he was in power, Chiang quarrelled with Chou and Mao, who broke away and set up a small communist state in a remote part of southern China in 1928. Chiang and his Nationalist army, as it was called, set about pacifying the whole country, by attacking all who opposed his government. He invaded the small communist state, and forced Mao to flee, with all of his followers to the wild north west of the country, a march of over nine thousand kilometres. Nevertheless they continued to resist the Nationalists until 1937.

By 1929 Chiang Kai-shek had done what Dr. Sun had dreamed: he had made his capital at Pekin and China was more or less one united country. There were still troublesome barons and bandits who had to be hunted down and executed, but for nearly eight years there was something like peace in a nation which had been torn with revolution and civil war for almost thirty years.

Just when all seemed settled, the Japanese, desperate to seize more territory, invaded north China from Manchuria, which they had captured six years earlier (see the map on page 87). Chiang Kai-shek and his Nationalists came to an agreement with Mao and the communists that they would forget their own quarrel and unite to drive out the invaders. The Nationalists attacked from one side and the communists from the other, but both were driven further and further into the interior of the country, leaving the coast and the fertile areas to the Japanese. This war dragged on, tying down vast numbers of Japanese soldiers, until the atomic bombs dropped by the United States in 1945 put an end to the fighting.

When the Japanese surrendered, the communist armies took over their weapons, and immediately reopened their quarrel with Chiang Kai-shek. The Nationalist army was driven back until there was no room left for them on the mainland. In 1949 Chiang took his defeated remnants to the island of Formosa, now called Taiwan, which is smaller than Scotland, some 160 km off shore (see the map on page 87). There he lived until his death in 1975, still maintaining that he was the ruler of the whole of China, and that one day he would return to the mainland. Taiwan today, with United States help, has become a relatively prosperous industrial state.

Under the leadership of Chairman Mao and his able prime minister, Chou En-lai, who died in 1975, China went through a violent social revolution. The corruption and many of the abuses of the old regime were swept away and a series of five-year plans on the Russian model were put into operation to try to improve the primitive agriculture and especially to build up a new industrial state. The People's Republic has been hindered by droughts and floods and terrible harvests; by a bitter and continuing quarrel with the USSR, who withdrew all its technicians and engineers who were helping to create the industry; by great social upheavals such as the Cultural Revolution of 1966; and by immense technical and industrial effort to make nuclear weapons, which had taken much of the nation's resources. Nevertheless immense strides have been made.

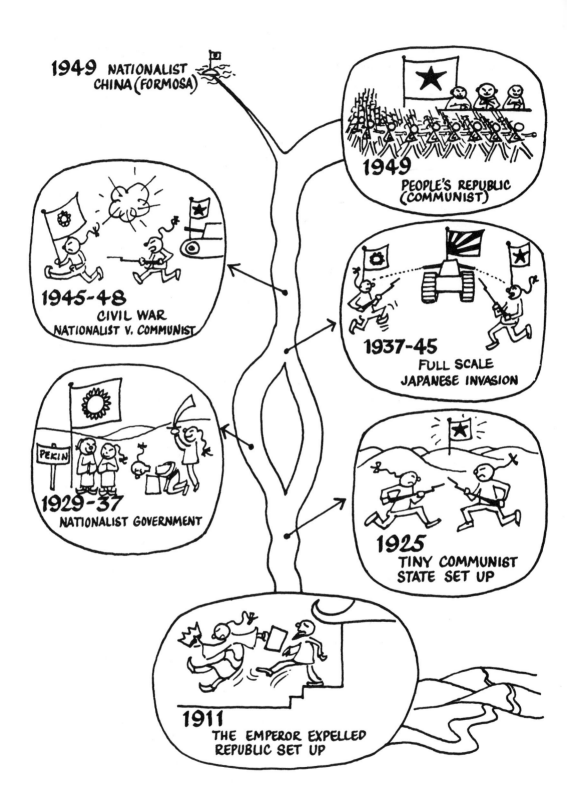

How the population of the countries may change between A.D. 1970–2000 if the present trends in the birth rate continue.

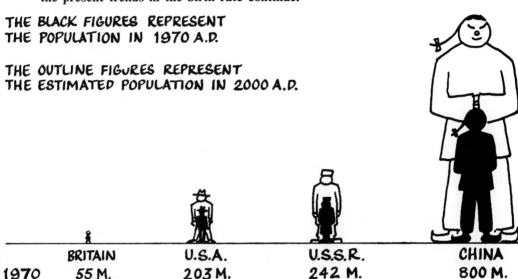

THE BLACK FIGURES REPRESENT
THE POPULATION IN 1970 A.D.

THE OUTLINE FIGURES REPRESENT
THE ESTIMATED POPULATION IN 2000 A.D.

	BRITAIN	U.S.A.	U.S.S.R.	CHINA
1970	55 M.	203 M.	242 M.	800 M.
2000	62 M.	290 M.	340 M.	1,000 M.

As Mao grew very old there were struggles inside the party for power, but the old leader kept most of the control in his own hands until he died in 1976. Immediately Hua Huo-feng, who was relatively little known outside China, became chairman.

The People's Republic of China forms a large proportion of the world's population, and by the year 2000 at the present rate of increase she will have 1,000,000,000 people, or almost twenty times the number of people in Britain. At the moment the People's Republic is underdeveloped and short of certain commodities, but in the future she will build more factories and become an up-to-date state. With all her huge population she must become one of the most powerful nations in the world, and how she will eventually behave is one of the great problems of the world today.

---

1. What made China ripe for rebellion at the beginning of the twentieth century?
2. What were the problems facing Dr. Sun in unifying China?
3. Who were the best-known of Dr. Sun's helpers? What has become of them today?
4. How did Chiang Kai-shek succeed where Dr. Sun failed?
5. Why did Chiang and Mao Tse-tung patch up their quarrel?
6. How did the resistance of the Chinese help the western allies in World War 2?

111

7. What important help did Mao have when he renewed his fight with Chiang and the Nationalists after the surrender of Japan in 1945?
8. Why is China so important in the world today?
9. Look at the chart on page 113 (British and Chinese products compared). Compared with Britain's, which are the largest industries in China, and which the smallest? Why do you think China is concentrating on the ones she is? Why do **you** think the output of motor vehicles is so small?

Find out:
(a) What was the Boxer rising?
(b) How many languages are there in China? How do you think this affects the government, the industry and the culture of the country?
(c) What offices did Mao Tse-tung and Chou En-lai hold in the Chinese People's Republic?
(d) Who is the deputy President of China?
(e) China now has nuclear power. What effect do you think this will have on her relations with the rest of the world?
(f) China is desperately poor and is short of everything except people. Why do you think her leaders have spent millions of pounds they can ill afford on developing an atom bomb?
(g) Find out what changes have occurred in China since 1949 in the fields of (a) communications, (b) industry, (c) agriculture, (d) relations with foreign countries.
(h) What is a commune in the Chinese sense of the word and how has this system helped China's agriculture?

Britain and China compared in size, population and production of important goods (1958 figures). This shows how much China is still behind a relatively small country such as Britain.

	BRITAIN	CHINA
POPULATION	55 MILLION	800 MILLION
EMPLOYMENT	2 OUT OF EVERY 100 WORKERS IN AGRICULTURE	80 OUT OF EVERY 100 WORKERS IN AGRICULTURE
AREA	234,000 km²	10,000,000 km²
STEEL	23 M. TONNES	24 M. TONNES
CEMENT	18 M. TONNES	33 M. TONNES
CHEMICAL FERTILISER	1,650,000 TONNES	25 M. TONNES
ELECTRICITY	250,000 M. KW.	100,000 M. KW.
PAPER	4 M. TONNES	2·5 M. TONNES
COAL	140 M. TONNES	420 M. TONNES

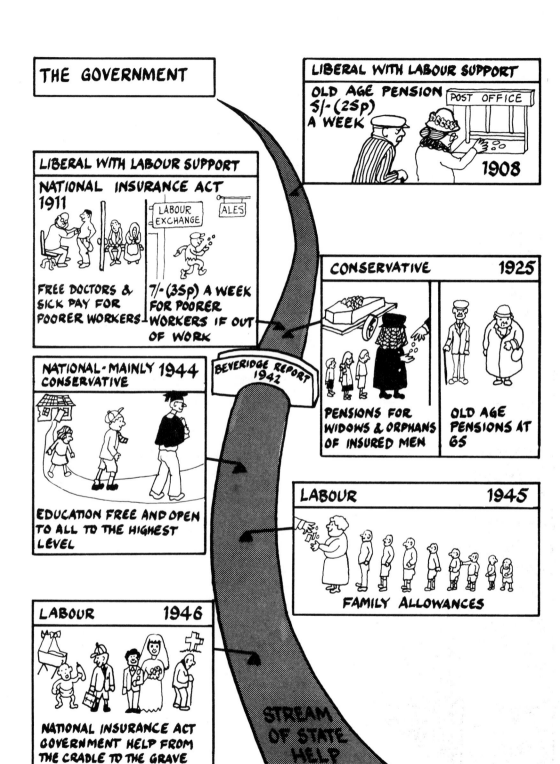

16

THE GROWTH
OF THE WELFARE STATE

The Welfare State is the means whereby the government makes sure that everyone is secure—or safe—from poverty, in illness and old age, and in any other misfortune which might happen to them. It means that no one shall be deprived of food, shelter, clothing, medical care, education or any of the essentials of a civilised life because he cannot afford them. Although we take this for granted today, it is only very recently that it has come about. Until the twentieth century it was generally agreed that every man should look after himself and his family, and that if he was ill or out of work, it was either bad management or bad luck. In neither case did the government consider that it should do much to help. The churches and some wealthy private people did try to help the poor and those in trouble, but charity could not, of course, give enough to everyone who needed it. In the nineteenth century many families joined clubs called friendly societies and paid in a few pence each week so that they could get a little help when misfortune struck them, and although this did help a little, it was far from sufficient.

SOCIAL (IN)SECURITY BEFORE THE TWENTIETH CENTURY

The first real step was taken by the Liberal government (helped by the small Labour party) in 1908 when it passed the Old Age Pension Act. This gave a maximum of 5/– (25p) a week to people over 70 years of age who had an income of less than £31·50 a year. Although this was not much, it did show that the government had at last realised that it had a responsibility

115

towards the less fortunate people of the country, and that when a man had spent his whole life working, he could not just be forgotten and left to die when he was no longer able to perform his normal job.

Three years later, in 1911, another step forward was taken when a re-elected Liberal government passed Mr. Lloyd George's National Insurance Act. Under the first part of this Act people earning under £160 a year could be insured against sickness. Each male worker paid 4d. (2p) a week, each woman worker 3d. (1½p), the employer another 3d. (1½p), and the government contributed 2d. (1p) for each person. Special stamps were stuck on insurance cards to show the money had been paid and, in return, the workers were allowed to have free medical treatment. Men were given 10/– (50p) a week and women 7s. 6d. (38p) if they could not work through illness.

The second part of the Act brought workers in trades such as building, engineering and shipbuilding, where there was a serious risk of unemployment because of the weather or trade changes, into an insurance scheme against unemployment. Again this scheme was based on contributions from employees, employers and the government. Workers were allowed 7s. 6d. (38p) a week if they were unemployed for a maximum of fifteen weeks in one year. During the next 30 years the scheme was extended until it covered everyone earning less than £8 per week. The benefits increased as the cost of living rose.

In 1925 the Conservative government under Baldwin took another important step. The contributions to the Health Insurance Scheme were increased and, out of this extra money, old-age pensions were to be paid to men over sixty-five and women over sixty. The government also decided to look after another group of unfortunate people. In future pensions were to be paid under the scheme to widows and orphans of insured men. The government's proposals were announced by Winston Churchill in his budget speech and were warmly approved by all parties in the House of Commons.

In 1942, right in the middle of World War 2, just when one would have expected it least, a committee headed by Sir William Beveridge made a report on what it thought the government should do about looking after the welfare of the whole nation when the war had been won. This report said that the state should make sure that no-one in the country suffered because of old age, illness, unemployment or any other misfortune, or because he had a large family. At the time, however, with the struggle against Germany and Japan costing many millions of pounds a day, nothing could be done until 1948.

Another step was taken in the passing of the Education Act of 1944. Among many other things, this abolished all fees in state schools, which meant that the poorest child could have the finest education—even the universities were free if the parents could not afford to pay. The leaving age was to be raised to fifteen, partly to give all children a much fairer chance in life. This was actually enforced in 1947.

In 1946 the newly-elected Labour government passed the National Insurance Act, much of which was based on the Beveridge Report. This made all medical treatment—doctors, hospitals, ambulances, dentists, and opticians—free to all who wanted it. Pensions to old people, disabled people and many other handicapped groups were increased, and those who were very poor but did not qualify for any of the normal pensions could get help from the National Assistance Board. To help parents with large families, allowances were paid by the government for every child under 16 after the first.

All of this naturally costs a great deal of money—well over £7,000,000,000 a year in 1975—and the sum increases every year. Some of this comes from taxes and some from the contributions that everyone over school age has to make. These depend on several factors, but in general anyone at work who earns £11 a week will pay 60p and the employer 93p, whereas someone earning £69 will pay £3·80 a week and the employer £5·85 (1975 figures).

Benefits of the welfare state
There is almost no-one in the country who is not helped in one way or another at some time in his life by the government's social security schemes. It starts even before the person is born: his mother gets free treatment and advice at the ante-natal clinics, and is given low price milk and special foods (free in some cases). When the baby is born, hospital and nursing is free, and she is given maternity grants of up to about £225 for women who are working.

The baby then has free treatment at the clinic, and cheap milk, foods and vitamins are available. When he is five years old he has a free education, with (in some counties) free transport by bus or taxi if he lives more than 3 miles from the school. Every day while he is in the infants' school he can have a bottle of milk free or at very low cost. School meals are provided for all pupils at less than the price they cost to produce, or for those who cannot afford even this, school dinners are free. Until he leaves school dental treatment and spectacles are free, and if he is unfortunate enough to need expensive education in a special school because he is blind, deaf or disabled, this costs his parents nothing.

When he grows up there are even more benefits waiting for him. He still gets all medical treatment at a very reduced rate, even medicines costing many pounds a bottle and operations costing thousands of pounds. If after a long illness a patient needs to go away to a convalescent home, he can do so at the state's expense. If a person is permanently injured at work (or in war), is blind or is left a widow, a weekly pension is paid.

Adults do, however, have to pay something towards the cost of spectacles and dental treatment.

If a person is not working, either because he cannot get a job or because he is ill, he is paid unemployment or sickness pay, and if he can no longer follow his usual trade because of injury, blindness or because that particular trade is no longer needed, he can be trained for another kind of work in special government training centres.

People who are really in trouble—for example, a woman whose husband has gone away and left her with a number of small children—and who are not eligible for any of the normal pensions, can get a certain weekly payment, according to their needs, from the Supplementary Benefits Scheme. Family Allowance is paid to all mothers, who get £4 a week for each child.

Old people again have many extra benefits on top of those that everyone else receives. They receive a weekly retirement pension at 60 or 65, and for those who are unable to look after themselves there are old people's homes. If elderly people do not wish to leave their own houses they can obtain help with the housework and sometimes get hot meals brought to them by van every day. Finally, when the person dies, the nearest relation can get a grant of up to £30 to help with the funeral expenses.

But these are only some of the welfare services: in fact the government tries to see that no-one is in need at any time of his life. So when you start work and notice on your pay slip each week the words 'Deduct National Insurance contributions' just think of all that you have had, and are going to get, for this. It is perhaps the best value in the world!

---

1. Find out when the Salvation Army was founded and by whom. (Look up BOOTH, William, in the Oxford Junior Encyclopaedia.) Make notes and give good reasons for its foundation.
2. What was the first important act of Parliament towards a Welfare State after 1900?
3. What help did the National Insurance Act of 1911 give to working people?
4. Who introduced the 1911 National Insurance Act, and where did the money for the benefits from this act come from?
5. What were the main recommendations of the Beveridge Report?
6. What new benefits did the Labour Government of 1945–50 add to the Welfare State?
7. The Welfare State is said to look after a person from his cradle to his grave. Show how this is true by mentioning different benefits a person may receive at different stages in his life.
8. It is sometimes said nowadays that the State is doing too much for the people, that as we live in an affluent society such things as free milk,

free medical service, family allowances and allied benefits are no longer necessary. Do you agree with this view? Do you think that as people are earning more and more money today there is no need to provide these benefits? Is it, for instance, true that no-one today lives on or near the poverty line?

Find out:
Note: In order to answer these questions it might be necessary to collect pamphlets on the subjects from the Post Office, the Careers Advisory Service, and the Department of Employment which give details of allowances, benefits and unemployment benefits.
(a) What National Insurance contributions will you pay when you leave school and start work?
(b) What contributions will your father be paying now?
(c) How much (i) sickness pay, and (ii) unemployment pay would you receive if you fell ill or were out of work within twelve months of leaving school?
(d) How much in family allowances would a woman be paid if she had five children aged 18, 14, 11, 6 and 3 months respectively?
(e) How much Old Age Pension does (i) a single person, (ii) a married couple receive?

17

THE COMMONWEALTH
IN THE 20th CENTURY

The Commonwealth is perhaps one of the most unusual, but the best, ways of uniting widely differing countries the world has ever seen. Nations of different colour, different religions, different languages and completely different ways of life have come together voluntarily to help each other and to settle problems of all kinds that concern them. The members of the Commonwealth have signed no treaties or alliances with each other: they do not even have a single person who is recognised as the head of all of the countries. They support many different political parties: they seem to have nothing which would be considered binding in normal relations between countries—yet the Commonwealth for the most part works well.

The old British Empire of the nineteenth century was made up of some countries which had been captured in war (Canada and parts of India, for example), some which had been discovered or explored by Britons (Australia, New Zealand, parts of Africa) and even some which had been bought (Singapore). These territories were ruled by the British government as colonies—that is, as their own property. The British Queen was their Queen, the British government made their laws, and the British army and courts kept them in order. The colonies provided a large and captive market for British goods and were a source of raw materials and cheap food. But all the time the people of the colonies were being trained to run their own affairs, first of all as ordinary soldiers, policemen and clerks, and then as officers and more important officials. Canada, Australia, New Zealand and South Africa were the first to be allowed a colonial government to run home affairs, such as education, agriculture and industry, while London still controlled such important affairs as taxation and defence. Then gradually the colonial governments took over these too, until, beginning with Canada, they were allowed complete freedom.

By 1976, 52 territories, once colonies, had been allowed independence. Of these, only four major states (Eire, Burma, Pakistan and South Africa) chose to leave the Commonwealth. The rest have asked to be allowed to remain closely linked with Britain to form the Commonwealth. Some of these countries still look on the Queen as their head: others (for example, India, Pakistan, Ghana, Nigeria, Uganda, Tanzania, Cyprus and Malaysia) have decided to become republics with an elected president as

THE EMPIRE – 19TH CENTURY. THE EMPIRE WAS LARGELY REGARDED AS A MARKET FOR BRITISH GOODS AND AS A SOURCE OF CHEAP RAW MATERIALS.

MANUFACTURED GOODS FOR COLONIES

CHEAP RAW MATERIALS FROM COLONIES

THE COMMONWEALTH – LATE 20TH CENTURY. AN ASSOCIATION, OR CLUB, OF EQUALS REGARDLESS OF COLOUR OR RELIGION.

their head of state, but still wish to belong to the Commonwealth in every other respect.

Although the countries of the Commonwealth are so different in many ways, they do have some things in common. Many, for example, have a system of government very much like the Houses of Parliament in Westminster, and carry out elections much as we do in Britain. All of them

have courts and police modelled on the British legal system: some still even use the courts in London as the final appeal for important cases. Many of the Commonwealth countries play British games—one has only to see the Indians, West Indians, Australians, or New Zealanders playing Test matches, or such different races as the Welsh and the Fijians battling on the rugby field to realise this. Many of the Commonwealth countries

123

speak English as well as their own language: in fact, in some countries such as India, where there are perhaps 400 different languages, often the only way a man from one part can speak to another is by using English.

Perhaps the most important link of all between the Commonwealth countries is the Prime Ministers' Conference, which is held at frequent intervals, often in London. Here the Prime Ministers and their advisers discuss problems which affect the Commonwealth, or even just a few of its members, and although they cannot pass any laws or give direct orders, they usually arrive at a solution or a settlement by agreement, which is a much more civilised way of conducting international affairs.

How the Commonwealth helps its members

1. Most Commonwealth countries give their people British citizenship. This makes it much easier to travel from one Commonwealth country to another as not so many documents have to be taken.
2. The Commonwealth countries, especially the older ones, help younger ones with loans of money for development. In war, many Commonwealth countries send soldiers to help any other member in trouble.
3. Ministers and other officials from Commonwealth countries meet to discuss their problems and help each other with difficulties.

---

1. The old idea of the British Empire has vanished entirely and the word Commonwealth taken its place. In what ways does the Commonwealth differ from the old British Empire?
2. Which was the first colony, apart from the United States, to obtain independence from Britain?
3. Quite simply state what is the purpose of the Prime Ministers' Conference.
4. The members of the Commonwealth fall into two groups with respect to their relationships to the Queen. What are these two groups and which countries are members of each?
5. What have most members of the Commonwealth in common?
6. As though you were a member of a Commonwealth country, write a letter to a friend in Europe explaining why you think it is better to be a member of the Commonwealth rather than a citizen in a fully independent country, completely separate from Britain.
7. What is a tariff? Show how tariffs in Britain used to work in favour of Commonwealth countries.
8. Suppose you were to travel around the world. Why would it be much easier to go via the countries of the Commonwealth?
9. Plan a trip round the world. You wish, however, to save money, so you

decide only to stop in Commonwealth countries. Make a list of the places at which you would stop and check that they are members of what has been called the British Family of Nations. In what ways would you (a), save money, and (b) save documentation?

Find out:
(a) Make a list of all members of the Commonwealth and find out how each came to be a member of the old British Empire. List your answers under the following headings:
(i) Captured in war; (ii) discovered or explored; (iii) bought; (iv) otherwise gained.
(b) Many small islands and small areas of land are still British colonies and although they are members of the Commonwealth, they do not have full independence. Find out the names of these and mark them on a map of the world.
(c) What are each of the following:
(i) a Dominion; (ii) a Protectorate; (iii) a Colony; (iv) a Mandated territory; (v) condominium. (Use both dictionaries and encyclopaedias for this question.)

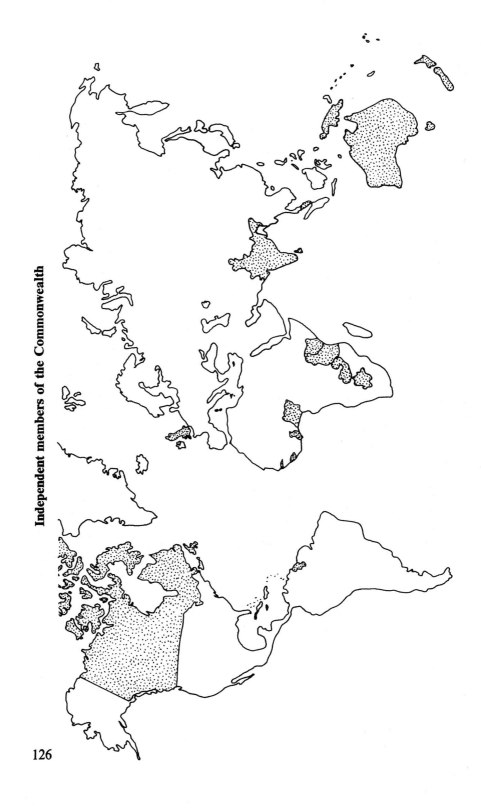

Independent members of the Commonwealth

18

THE UNITED STATES OF EUROPE

Uniting for war

When World War 2 ended nearly all of the countries of Europe were left poor and weak. The United States of America and Russia had become the most powerful nations on earth. But neither the U.S.A. nor the U.S.S.R. is really a single country as France or Norway or England is: they are gigantic countries made up of a number of smaller, partly-independent states. The U.S.A. consists of 50 separate states, each with its own government for making state laws, but with a single central government in Washington and one President for all of them. The state governments make the laws for their own states dealing with such things as crime, education, licensing, employment, divorce and voting, but the central government is responsible for the more important decisions, such as taxation, defence and foreign relations, for the whole of the U.S.A. In the same way the U.S.S.R. is made up of 15 separate republics, each with its own president and government, but with one central government in Moscow to decide the more important matters for all of the fifteen. The countries of Europe each have their own kings, queens or presidents and their own governments to make their own laws quite independently.

After the war, for their own protection, most of the European states signed defence treaties with one of the two 'giants'. Britain, Belgium, France. Western Germany. Norway. Italy. Holland. Portugal, Iceland, Luxemburg, Greece and Turkey decided to join the United States and Canada in the North Atlantic Treaty Organisation (NATO), while Poland, Eastern Germany, Hungary, Czechoslovakia, Bulgaria, Rumania and Albania joined Russia in the Warsaw Pact.

Each member of NATO puts part of its army, navy and air force into a single defence force under a single general from one of the countries to fight anyone who might attack any of the member states. You could find a NATO fleet made of British, French, American and Dutch warships under the command of a German admiral. The Warsaw Pact countries have a similar arrangement for their members.

But NATO and the Warsaw Pact are designed for war only, and everyone hopes that because of the United Nations there will be no more war. A strong feeling is growing that the countries of Europe should unite, not only for warlike reasons, but also for peaceful ones. Many politicians look forward to a United States of Europe just as there is a United States of America or a Union of Soviet Socialist Republics.

Uniting for peace

The United States of Europe is a dream, but there are many difficulties in the way. Each country has its own language, its own money and its own traditions which it will not like to give up. The way of life of a family from southern Italy for example, will be very different from that of a family in northern Norway. Wages, even for men doing the same job, vary a great deal between the different countries: a German miner will get perhaps three or four times the wages of a Spanish miner who probably works longer hours.

Then there is the problem of a single government for all of Europe. The present rulers, presidents, prime ministers and monarchs might be unwilling to give up any of their power to a foreigner. In a European parliament there might be problems over the number of members each state should have. Should a large country like Western Germany with 62 million people have the same number of representatives as Luxemburg which has only 348,000 inhabitants?

These are only a few of the many problems, but if they could be solved there would be immense advantages. First of all, the United States of Europe with 300 million people would be a very powerful nation indeed. Then, if customs duties were abolished, as they would be inside a single country, goods would be much cheaper. For countries not so fortunate as the others, there would be a rise in the standard of living. In Spain, for example, education is compulsory only from the ages of 6–13, and in Portugal, where in 1950 one person in every three could neither read nor write, children must attend school only from the ages of 7–13.

If all of Europe were a single country travel would be much easier as there would be no passports, travel documents or customs barriers. And when people travel more easily, ideas travel more rapidly too, so that whereas each separate country now has scientists and engineers working on the same problems of medicine and industry, in a United States of Europe these secrets could be shared by all.

A small beginning

A small beginning was made in 1957 when by the Treaty of Rome France, Western Germany, Italy, Belgium, the Netherlands and Luxemburg set up the European Economic Community (EEC) or Common Market. These six countries agreed to abolish all customs duties among each other gradually, to make it easier to travel from one to the other and to share each other's iron, steel, coal and atomic energy. They hope that by joining together first of all for trade they will later join as one state politically.

In 1959 seven other European countries not belonging to the Common Market (Britain, Austria, Denmark, Norway, Portugal, Sweden and

128

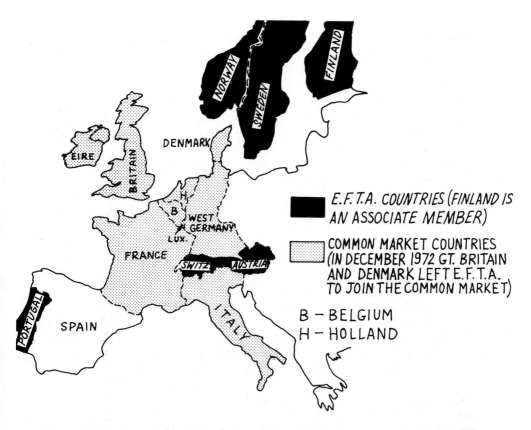

E.F.T.A. COUNTRIES (FINLAND IS AN ASSOCIATE MEMBER)

COMMON MARKET COUNTRIES (IN DECEMBER 1972 GT. BRITAIN AND DENMARK LEFT E.F.T.A. TO JOIN THE COMMON MARKET)

B – BELGIUM
H – HOLLAND

Switzerland) signed the Convention of Stockholm to set up the European Free Trade Area (EFTA) which also planned to abolish customs duties between member states.

The Conservative government in 1963 and the Labour government in 1967 engaged in negotiations for Britain to join the Common Market, but on both occasions the application was vetoed by General de Gaulle who believed that Britain would not increase taxes on Commonwealth products and that British agricultural methods would not suit the EEC. (British agriculture was the most efficient in the world and the French one of the most inefficient in Europe). De Gaulle also had a personal dislike of Britain and was perhaps afraid that if she was admitted France might lose the leadership of the Common Market.

However, after de Gaulle's death Britain applied once more for membership and Britain, together with Eire, Denmark and Norway, were invited to begin negotiations to enter the Common Market in 1970. The long and difficult negotiations with all four countries were completed by June 1972. Norway then held a referendum in which the people voted to stay out of the Common Market so she withdrew her application. Britain, Eire and Denmark became members on January 1st 1973.

However, when the Labour government came into power it insisted on renegotiating the terms of entry accepted by the Conservative Prime Minister, Edward Heath. After these negotiations were completed, the Labour government held a referendum in June 1975—the first in the country's history—and the figures showed a two to one majority in favour of the Common Market.

Since then relationships between Britain and her fellow members have not always been easy but most people do think, that although there are many problems, the advantages do outweigh the disadvantages.

U.S.A.   W. EUROPE   U.S.S.R.

Size and population of the three compared
This shows how densely populated the countries of Western Europe are when compared with the United States or Russia.

	Area	Population
U.S.A.	9,400,000 km²	200,000,000
W. Europe	2,600,000 km²	320,000,000
U.S.S.R.	22,500,000 km²	240,000,000

1. How do the United States of America and the U.S.S.R. differ from Britain, France or China? (*politically*, not in size, language or race)
2. Why do you think the central (or federal) government of the U.S.A. and the U.S.S.R. controls defence, finance and foreign affairs, instead of allowing each state or republic to manage its own?
3. Why did Europe divide itself into two groups after the war?
4. What were the names of these groups, and what is their main purpose?
5. What advantages would there be if the nations of Europe could unite into the United States of Europe?
6. What disadvantages might there be from such a union?
7. What is the Common Market, and which countries belong to it?
8. What is EFTA, and which countries are members?

130

THE UNITED STATES OF EUROPE

THE DIFFICULTIES AND DRAWBACKS

THE REWARDS

DIFFERENT LANGUAGES,

TEN PENCE   DIX FRANCS   CINCO PESETAS   CENTO LIRE

WEIGHTS AND MONEY

MUCH MORE POWERFUL

DIFFERENT OUTLOOKS

AND WAYS OF LIFE

NO TAX £2 £1.50   NO DUTY £2,000 £1,800

MOST GOODS CHEAPER

DIFFERENT WAGES AND

WAGES

STANDARDS OF LIVING

LEVELLING UP OF WAGES

WAGES   WAGES   WAGES   WAGES

AND STANDARDS

WESTERN GERMANY

62,000,000 PEOPLE

LUXEMBOURG

348,000 PEOPLE

DIFFERENT SIZES

EASIER COMMUNICATION –

FRANCE   GERMANY

– ONE COUNTRY TO ANOTHER

TO LET PARLIAMENT BUILDINGS SUITABLE FOR SCHOOL OR OFFICE

LOSS OF INDIVIDUAL SOVEREIGNTY

LESS WASTE ON RESEARCH AND EXPERIMENT

9. What is the average density of population (that is, the number of people per square kilometre) in the U.S.A., the U.S.S.R., and Western Europe? Draw three squares, 4 cm each side, to represent one square kilometre of America, Russia and Western Europe. Put one dot for each person per square kilometre in the squares.

Find out:
10. What do SEATO and CENTO stand for? Which countries are members of these organisations?
11. Find out the two main products of each of the countries of Western Europe, and suggest what

Britain could send to France,	Spain could send to Norway,
France could send to Britain,	Norway could send to Portugal,
Britain could send to Italy,	Portugal could send to Denmark,
Italy could send to Britain,	Denmark could send to Sweden,
Germany could send to Spain,	Sweden could send to Belgium,

if all of these countries were members of a customs-free United States of Europe.

19
THE 20th CENTURY
A PICTURE SUMMARY

These are some of the differences between your life today* and that of your great-grandparents (column 1) and your grandparents (column 2).

1905 – 10	1935 – 37	TODAY
YOU WOULD PROBABLY HAVE BEEN ONE OF A FAMILY OF...		
OF EVERY 1,000 BABIES BORN, THESE WOULD HAVE BEEN DEAD BEFORE ONE YEAR...		
125	58	21
IF YOU REACHED THE AGE OF 1 YOU COULD EXPECT TO LIVE TO THE AGE OF...		
53 56	58 61	69 74 years
YOU WOULD BE COMPELLED TO GO TO SCHOOL FROM THE AGE OF 5 UNTIL...		
12 YEARS	14 YEARS	16 YEARS

* Figures given are for 1976

1905-10	1935-37	TODAY

THIS IS HOW MOTOR CARS WERE SHARED OUT AMONG THE POPULATION...

1 FOR 8-900 PEOPLE | 1 FOR EVERY 20-30 PEOPLE | 1 FOR EVERY 4 PEOPLE

YOU WOULD SAVE HARD WHEN MARRIED TO BUY THESE LUXURIES FOR YOUR FAMILY...

FRIDGE | WASH

THESE WOULD BE YOUR MAIN AMUSEMENTS IN ADDITION TO SPORTS, RACING, ETC. ...

CYCLING
THEATRE
PUBLIC HOUSE MUSIC INDOOR GAMES

HIKING
CINEMA
RADIO DANCING

T.V.
CARS · MOTOR CYCLES
BINGO
MUSIC RECORDS GAMBLING

THIS IS HOW YOU WOULD BE LOOKED AFTER IN YOUR OLD AGE...

SAVINGS OR CHARITY | PENSIONS — SAVINGS & 50p WEEK PENSION | OLD FOLKS HOME PENSIONS NATIONAL HEALTH — PENSION & MANY BENEFITS

THESE ARE THE COMMONEST CAUSES OF DEATH AT THE TIME...

INFECTIOUS DISEASES CANCER T.B. HEART RESPIRATORY PNEUMONIA BRONCHITIS
7% 8% 10% 12% 17%

INFECTIOUS DISEASES T.B. RESPIRATORY CANCER HEART
2% 7% 10% 15% 25%

INFECTIOUS DISEASES T.B. RESPIRATORY CANCER HEART
1/3% 1/4% 13% 15% 43%

FOR FURTHER READING

(* before a book means that it is more difficult, but still worth looking at.)

GENERAL WORLD HISTORY

The 20th Century. M.N.Duffy. Blackwell.
The Momentous Years 1919–1958. H.E.Priestley and J.J.Betts. Dent.
An Atlas of World Affairs. A.Boyd. Methuen paperback.
Oxford Junior Encyclopaedia, Vol.5; Great Lives. Oxford University Press.
   (Good for brief biographies of famous people of the twentieth century)
Oxford Junior Encyclopaedia, Vol.10; Law and Order. Oxford University Press.
   (Details of the wars, political events, Communism, Nazism, etc.)
* *World History 1914–1961.* D.Thomson. Oxford University Press.
* *Background to Current Affairs.* D. Crowley. Macmillan.
   (Gives a good background to the development of Germany, Italy and USSR)
* *Dictionary of Modern History 1789–1945.* A.W.Palmer. Penguin.

BRITISH HISTORY

An Illustrated History of Modern Britain. D.Richards and J.W.Hunt. Longmans.
A Century of Change 1837–Today. R.J.Unstead. A. &. C.Black.
   (A simple text with many illustrations)
Portrait of Britain between the Exhibitions, 1851–1951. D.Lindsay and E.S.Washington. Oxford University Press.
History of Everyday Things in England 1851–1914. M. & C.H.B.Quennell. Batsford.
Twentieth Century Britain. A.Allen. Rockliff.
   (A straightforward account divided into topics. Many illustrations)
English Costume. D.Yarwood. Batsford.
   (Deals with costumes for men and women, accessories, hairstyles. Mainly drawings)
Visual History of Modern Britain series. Editor, J.Simmonds. Vista.
   The Town—G.Martin.
   Transport—J.Simmonds.
   The House and Home—M.W.Barley.
   Industry and Technology—W.H.Chaloner and A.E.Musson.
   Government—R.H.Evans.
   The Land—J.Higgs.
   (Each book has over 200 photographs and illustrations with long descriptive captions as well as text)
Suffragettes and Votes for Women. L.Snelgrove. Longmans.
Churchill and his World. A.Moorhead. Thames and Hudson.
   (The life and work of Winston S.Churchill as seen through photographs, cartoons and documents with linking text)
Aspirin Age 1919–41. Editor, E.Leighton. Penguin.
* *The Uses of Literacy.* R.Hoggart. Penguin.
(How the working class lived and amused themselves between the wars and in the 1940s)

THE UNITED NATIONS

The Story of The United Nations. K. Savage. Bodley Head.
How People work together. United Nations Department of Public Information.
Today is History series. Hart-Davis Educational.
    The United Nations. Katharine Savage.

USSR

The 'First' Books. Edmund Ward.
    The Soviet Union.
Today is History series. Hart-Davis Educational.
    Russia. Bryan Hammond.
Methuen Outline series. Methuen.
    Russia. J. Lawrence.
The Lands and Peoples series. A. & C. Black.
    USSR.
* *A Short History of Russia.* D. M. Sturley. Longmans.
* *Meet Soviet Russia.* J. Gunther. Hamish Hamilton.
Coco the Clown. N. Poliakoff (Coco of Bertram Mills' circus).
    Dent. (The life story of Coco, who was born in Russia and fought all through
    the war against the Germans and through the Russian Revolution)
The Making of Modern Russia. L. Viochan. Penguin.

USA

Today is History series. Hart-Davis Educational.
    Land of the Free, the USA.
The Lands and Peoples series. A. & C. Black.
    USA.
Everyday life in 20th Century America. J. W. Dodds. Batsford.
    (A well-illustrated account of American life, entertainment and advertising
    from 1900 to the present)
An Outline of American History. United States Information Service.
    (A well-illustrated book, free to schools from USIS)
A History of the U.S.A., Vols. I and II. R. B. Nye and J. E. Morpuiga. Penguin.

ASIA

* *The Rise of Modern Asia.* D. Thomson. Oxford University Press.
    (A fairly difficult book but well worth reading for an overall picture of Asia)
South East Asia in Turmoil. B. Crozier. Penguin.
The 'First' Books. Edmund Ward.
    China Today.
The Lands and Peoples series. A. & C. Black.
    China.
    Japan.
Great Revolutions series. Thames and Hudson.
    The Chinese Revolution.
    (Many excellent pictures—well worth seeing at your local library)
The Birth of Communist China. C. P. Fitzgerald. Penguin.

Hiroshima Diary. Michihiko Hachiya. Gollancz.
  (An eye-witness account of the dropping and aftermath of the first atomic
  bomb, by a Japanese doctor of a Hiroshima hospital)
A History of Modern Japan. R. Storry. Penguin.
A History of India, Vols. I and II. P. Spear. Penguin.

WORLD WAR I

Benn's Twentieth Century Histories. Ernest Benn.
  World War I. D. Scott-Daniel.
Picture Monographs. Hamish Hamilton.
  The Battle of Jutland. R. Hough.
  (The naval war)
  The Camel Fighter. J. Pudney.
  (The air war)
The First World War—an Illustrated History. A.J.P. Taylor. Hamish Hamilton.
  Also Penguin Books.
  (All of the four books above contain many photographs with linking text)
Methuen Outline series. Methuen.
  The First World War. R.R. Sellman.
  (Good clear outline with many drawings)

WORLD WAR II

Illustrated History of World War II. Edmund Ward. 16 volumes including:
  European Land Battles.   The Wolf Packs.
  Land Battles in the North.   The Air War in the West.
  Africa, Sicily and Italy.   Asiatic Land Battles.
  The Naval War in the West.   The Resistance.
                    World War II: a Summary.
  (All are very well illustrated with photographs)
Today is History series. Hart-Davis Educational.
  A State of War (Europe 1939–1945). Katharine Savage.
Methuen Outline series. Methuen.
  The Second World War. R.R. Sellman.
Benn's Twentieth Century Histories. Ernest Benn.
  World War 2. D. Scott-Daniel.

NOVELS ABOUT THE TWENTIETH CENTURY

Kipps. H.G. Wells. Collins.
The History of Mr. Polly. H.G. Wells. Collins.
  { Books about the lives of ordinary people before World War I.

The Admirable Crichton.
The Silver Box.
  { Plays by J. M. Barrie, John Galsworthy. Duckworth.
  (Deal with the upper classes and the class problem in the early years of the century)

Jeeves. (Or any of the Bertie Wooster novels.) P. G. Wodehouse. Barrie & Jenkins.
  (Caricatures of upper-class life in the 1920s)
The Citadel. A.J. Cronin. Gollancz.
  (Life between the wars)

Room at the Top. J. Braine. Eyre and Spottiswoode.
Saturday Night and Sunday Morning. A. Sillitoe. Secker & Warburg.
   (Both these deal with life in the 1950s and 1960s, especially in industrial towns)
The Cruel Sea. N. Monsarrat. Cassell.
   (The navy in World War II)
A Town like Alice. N. Shute. Heinemann.
   (War in the Far East)
The Wooden Horse. E. Williams. Collins.
   (Escape from prison camp)
The Good Earth. P. Buck. Methuen.
(China before the war)
For Whom the Bell Tolls. E. Hemingway. Cape.
(Spanish Civil War)

INDEX